Sadlier Discovering God Program

A Faith-Development Program for
Five-Year-Olds

Discovering God's Love
Songbook

by
Julie Brunet
and
Renée McAlister

William H. Sadlier, Inc.
9 Pine Street
New York, NY 10005–4700

Contents

Unit 1
Fall Unit Page
Fall Is Here.................................... 5

Lesson 1
My New Friends............................... 6

Lesson 2
Come Join Me 7
Shine Your Light 8
Praying (fingerplay)........................... 9

Lesson 3
Ten Helpful Fingers (fingerplay)............. 10

Lesson 4
Helping Hands 11

Lesson 5
People Who Care for Me...................... 12
I Am Growing (#1) 14

Lesson 6
Magic Carpet (poem) 15
Pumpkin, Pumpkin (poem).................... 18
Halloween Fun 16

Lesson 7
Thanksgiving Song............................ 19

Lesson 8
The Bible 20

Unit 2
Winter Unit Page
Winter's Here 21

Lesson 9
God's Great Big World 22
God Made Everything......................... 23

Lesson 10
See What I Can Do. 24
I Am Special 25

Lesson 11
An Activity Song 26
I'm Learning About My God 28
I Am Growing (#2) 29

Lesson 12
God Has a Plan 30

Lesson 13
Feelings 31

Lesson 14
Christmas Is Coming 32

Lesson 15
Christmas. 33

Unit 3
Spring Unit Page
Spring Is Here 34

Lesson 17
God Gave Me My Family 35
The Holy Family 36

Lesson 18
Helping (fingerplay). 37

Lesson 19
Showing Love. 38

Lesson 20
My Family. 40

Lesson 21
I Am Sorry 42

Lesson 22
Valentine's Day 43

Lesson 23
Eggs in a Nest 44
Creeping Crawling Caterpillar 45
Spinning a Cocoon 46
Easter 47
Pretty Butterfly 48

Lesson 24
Let It Shine 49

Unit 4
Summer Unit Page
Summer's Coming 50

Lesson 25
My Baptism 51

Lesson 26
The Bible (poem) 52

Lesson 27
I'm Learning How to Pray 53
We Pray to God 54

Lesson 28
We Celebrate the Mass 56

Lesson 29
Goodbye and Hello 58

Lesson 30
Mom 60
Dad 61

Lesson 31
Mary Our Mother 62

Lesson 32
A Birthday Song 63

Fall Is Here

To the tune of "Frère Jacques"

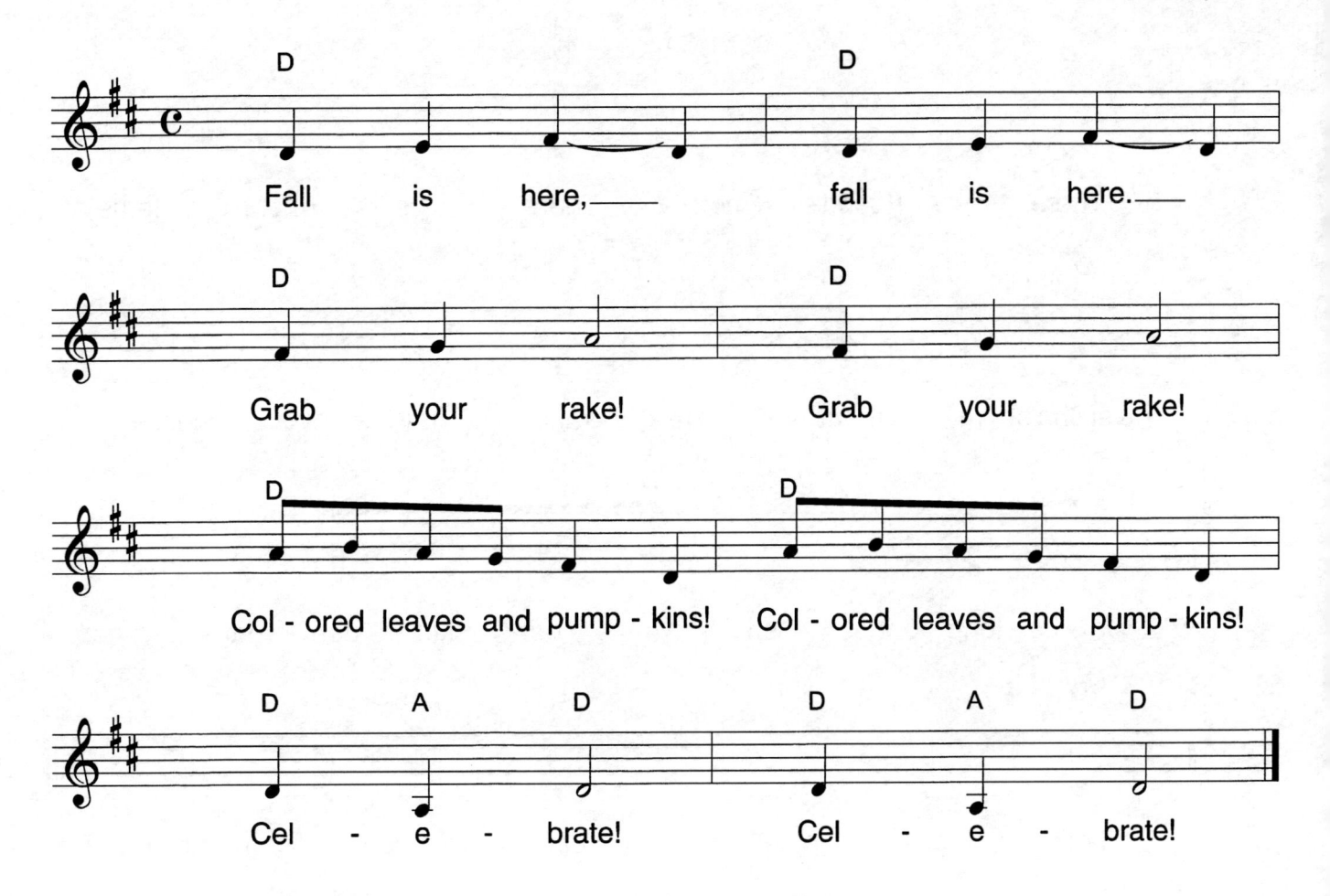

Fall is here, fall is here.
Grab your rake! Grab your rake!
Col-ored leaves and pump-kins! Col-ored leaves and pump-kins!
Cel-e-brate! Cel-e-brate!

Lesson 1, Part 1

My New Friends

To the tune of "Where Is Thumbkin?"

There is (friend's name). There is (friend's name).

He's(She's) my friend He's(She's) my friend.

We be-long to-geth-er In our kin-der-gar-ten.

Let's be friends. Let's be friends.

Discovering God's Love Songbook

Come Join Me

To the tune of
"The Farmer in the Dell"

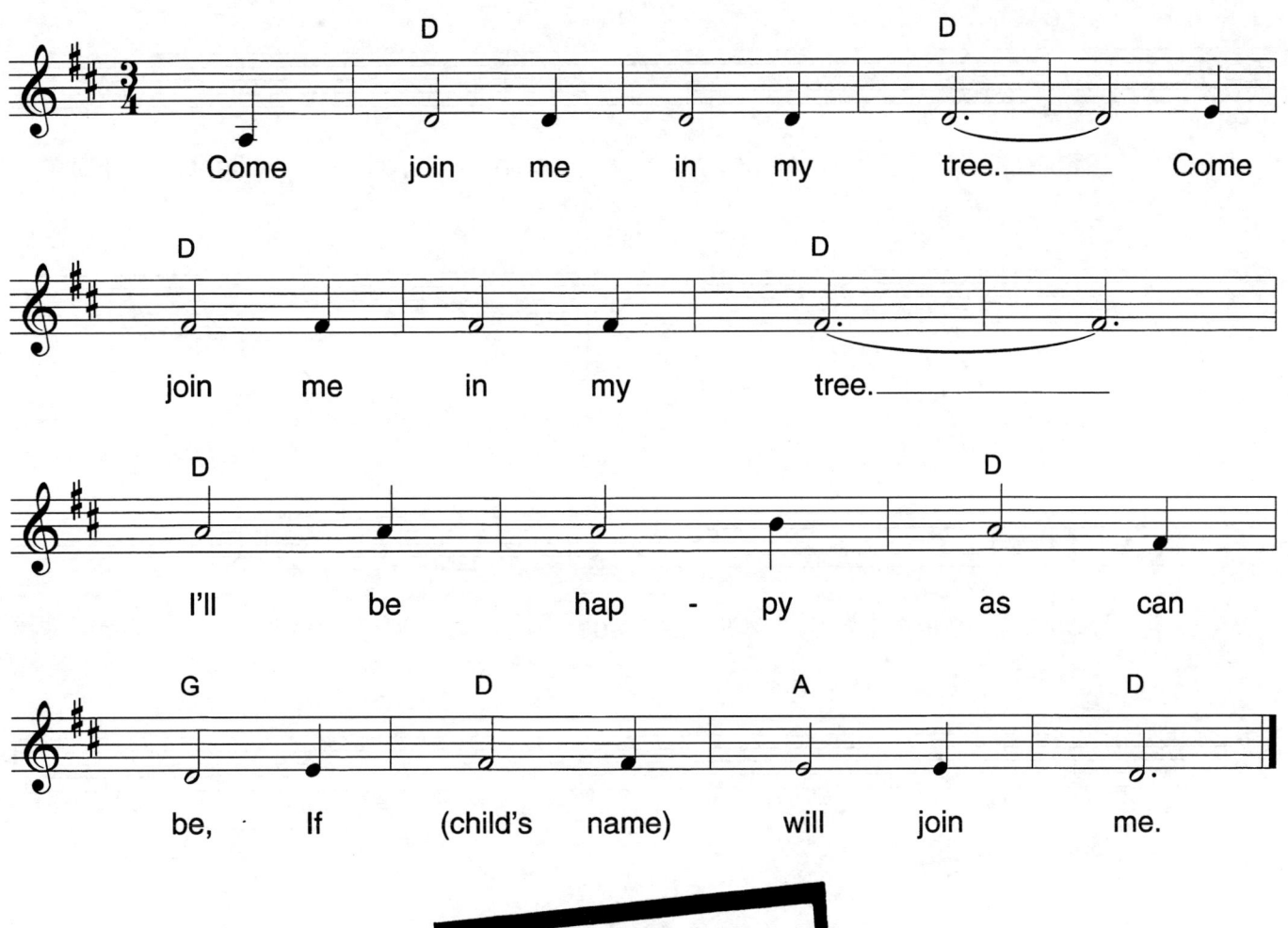

Come join me in my tree. Come
join me in my tree.
I'll be hap - py as can
be, If (child's name) will join me.

Sudie Squirrel is my brand new friend in my Kindergarten.

Discovering God's Love Songbook

Lesson 2, Part 3

Shine Your Light

*To the tune of
"Row, Row, Row Your Boat"*

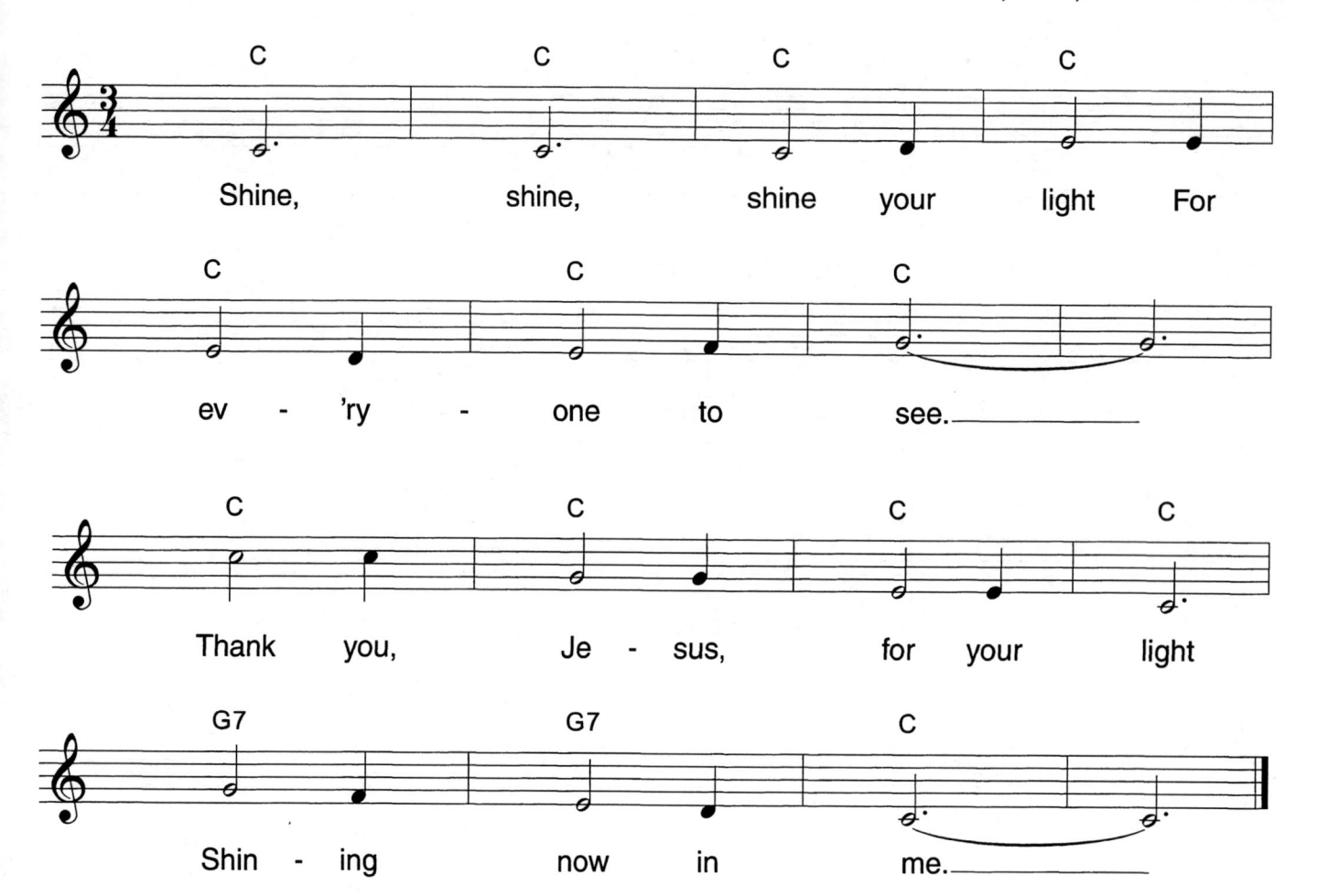

Shine, shine, shine your light For ev-'ry-one to see.

Thank you, Je-sus, for your light Shin-ing now in me.

8   Discovering God's Love Songbook

Praying
(fingerplay)

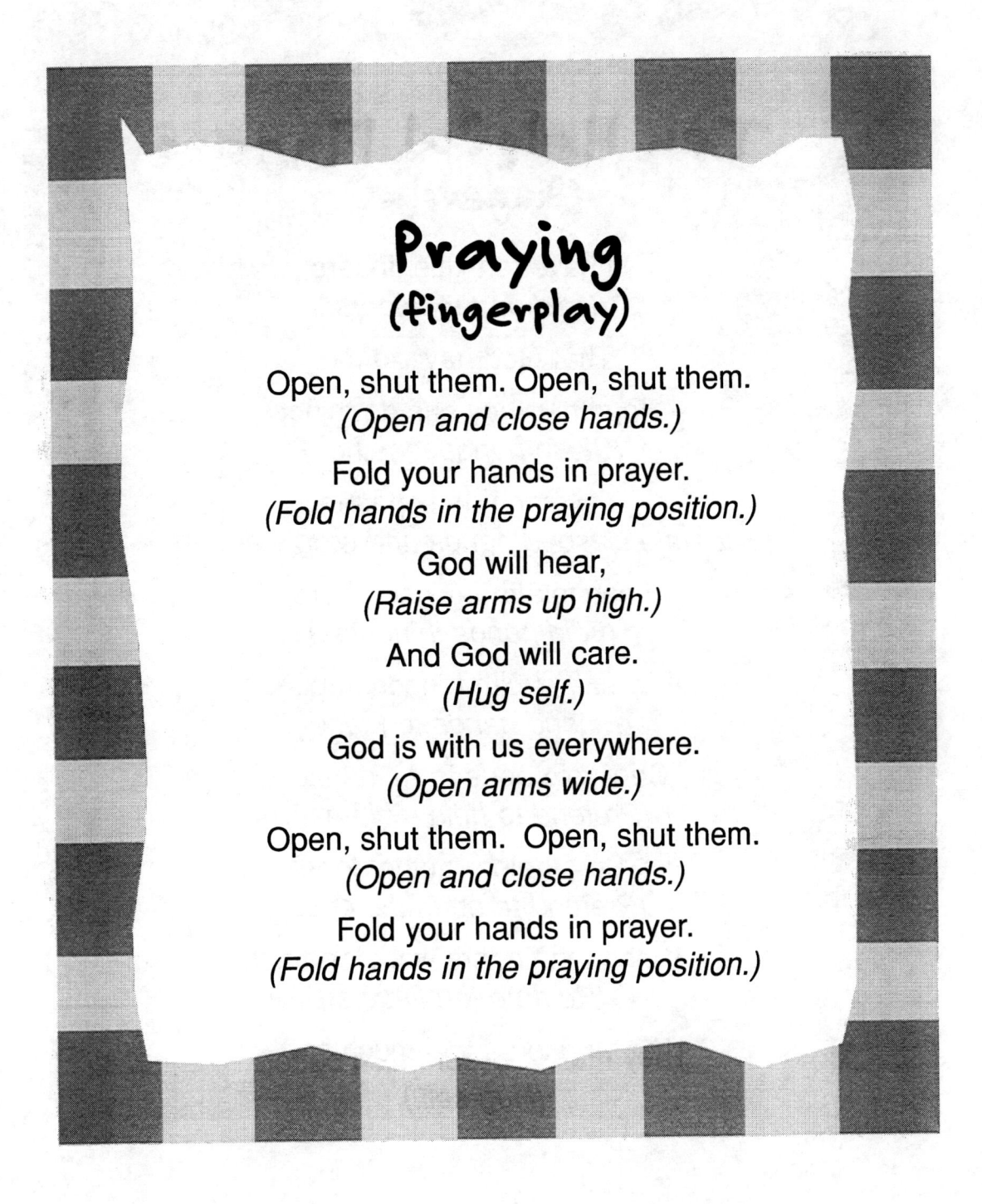

Open, shut them. Open, shut them.
(Open and close hands.)

Fold your hands in prayer.
(Fold hands in the praying position.)

God will hear,
(Raise arms up high.)

And God will care.
(Hug self.)

God is with us everywhere.
(Open arms wide.)

Open, shut them. Open, shut them.
(Open and close hands.)

Fold your hands in prayer.
(Fold hands in the praying position.)

Lesson 3, Part 3

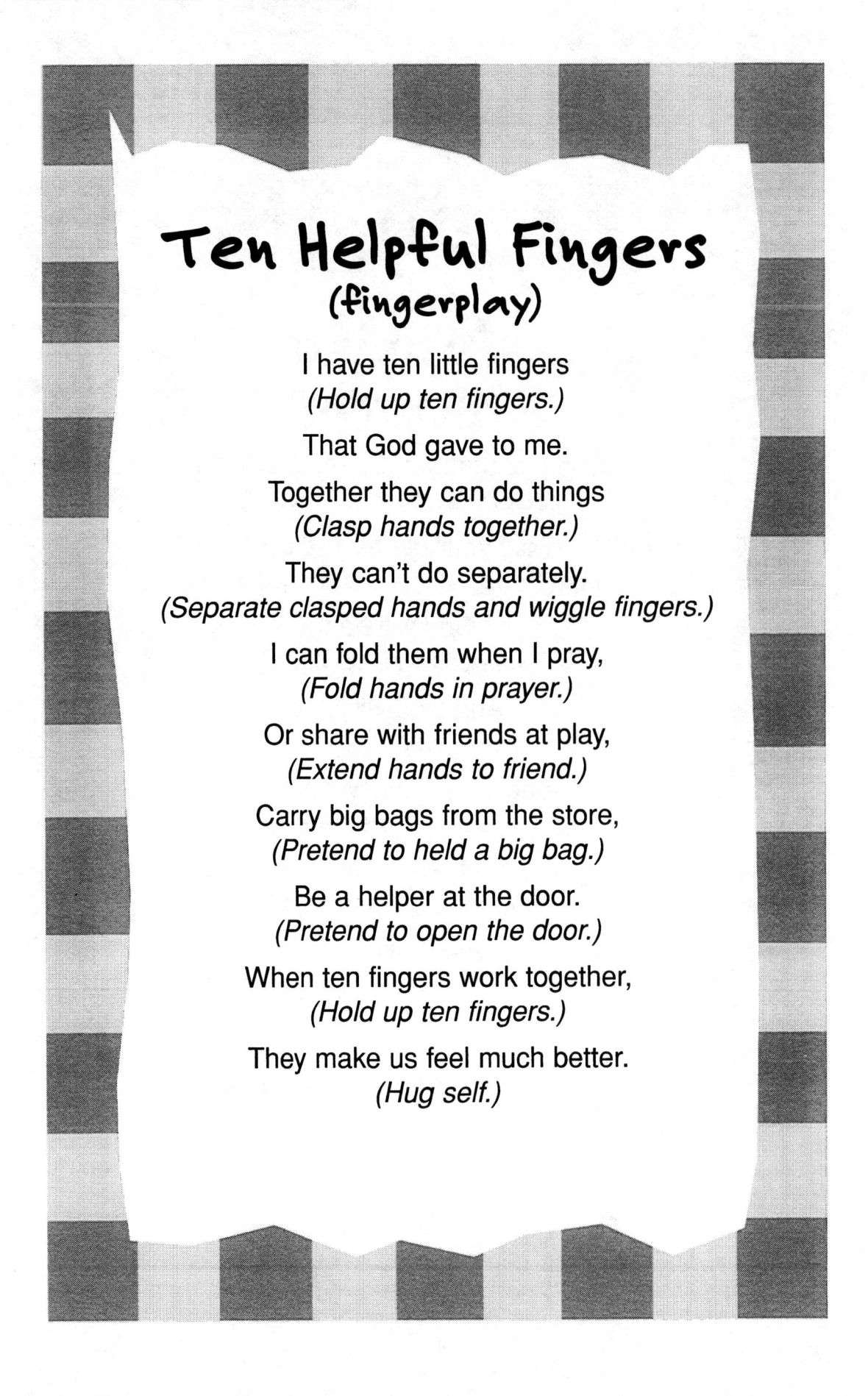

Ten Helpful Fingers
(fingerplay)

I have ten little fingers
(Hold up ten fingers.)

That God gave to me.

Together they can do things
(Clasp hands together.)

They can't do separately.
(Separate clasped hands and wiggle fingers.)

I can fold them when I pray,
(Fold hands in prayer.)

Or share with friends at play,
(Extend hands to friend.)

Carry big bags from the store,
(Pretend to held a big bag.)

Be a helper at the door.
(Pretend to open the door.)

When ten fingers work together,
(Hold up ten fingers.)

They make us feel much better.
(Hug self.)

ND# Helping Hands

To the tune of
"Here We Go 'Round the Mulberry Bush"

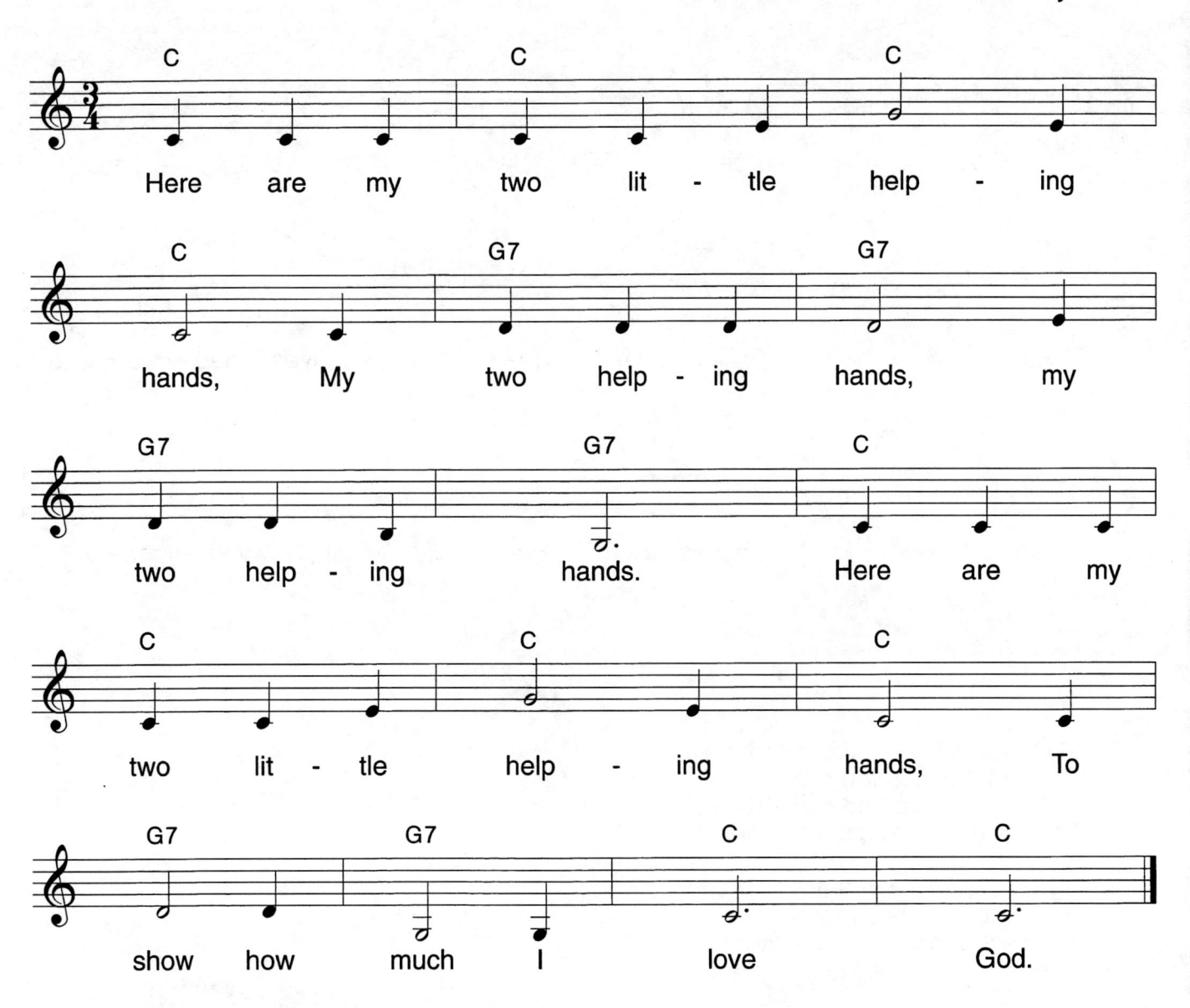

Here are my two lit - tle help - ing hands, My two help - ing hands, my two help - ing hands. Here are my two lit - tle help - ing hands, To show how much I love God.

2. I use my two hands in so many ways,
    In so many ways, in so many ways.
    I use my two hands in so many ways
    To show how much I love you.

Discovering God's Love Songbook

Lesson 5, Part 1 Extra! Extra!

People Who Care for Me

To the tune of "Mary Had a Little Lamb"

God gives peo-ple who care for me,
Care for me, Care for me.
God gives peo-ple who care for me.
They're a spe-cial gift, you see.

2. My parents love and comfort me,
   Comfort me, comfort me.
   My parents love and comfort me.
   They're a special gift, you see.

3. My teacher always reads to me,
   Reads to me, reads to me.
   My teacher always reads to me.
   She's (He's) a special gift, you see.

12 Discovering God's Love Songbook

4. The parish priest says Mass for me,
   Mass for me, Mass for me.
   The parish priest says Mass for me.
   He's a special gift, you see.

5. The farmer grows the food for me,
   Food for me, food for me.
   The farmer grows the food for me.
   He's (She's) a special gift, you see.

6. The doctor helps me when I'm sick,
   When I'm sick, when I'm sick.
   The doctor helps me when I'm sick.
   He's (She's) a special gift, you see.

7. The police officer keeps me safe from harm,
   Safe from harm, safe from harm.
   The police officer keeps me safe from harm.
   He's (She's) a special gift, you see.

Discovering God's Love Songbook

Lesson 5, Part 2

I Am Growing (#1)

*To the tune of
"Mary Had a Little Lamb"*

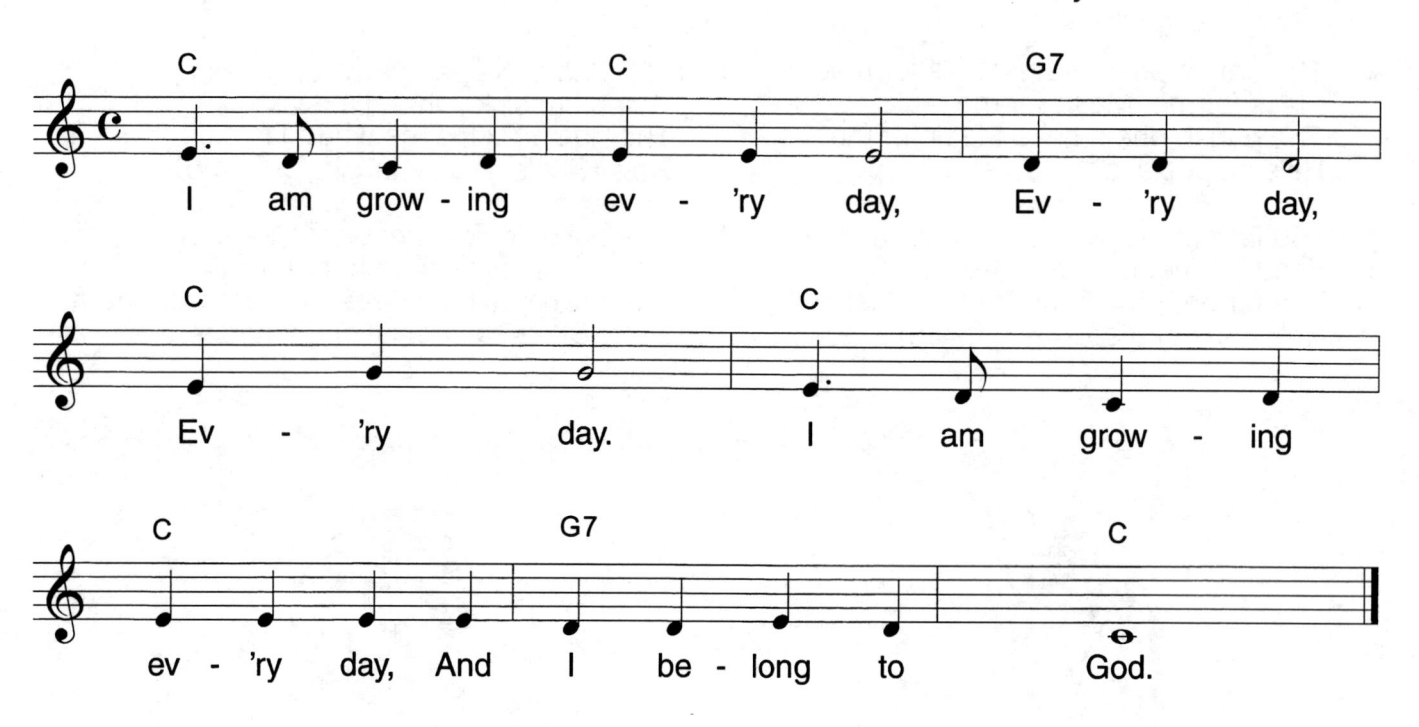

I am grow-ing ev-'ry day, Ev-'ry day, Ev-'ry day. I am grow-ing ev-'ry day, And I be-long to God.

2. I am learning whom to trust,
   Whom to trust, whom to trust.
   I am learning whom to trust,
   And all the safety rules.

I am a waitress in a restaurant.

14 Discovering God's Love Songbook

Magic Carpet
(poem)

Magic Carpet, take us today,
To a land that's far, far away
Where cowboys ride with hats so tall.
Take us, Magic Carpet, one and all.

Magic Carpet, take us today,
To a land that's far, far away
Where ballerinas on their toes stand tall.
Take us, Magic Carpet, one and all.

Magic Carpet, take us today,
To a land that's far, far away
Where a football player scores with a ball.
Take us, Magic Carpet, one and all.

Magic Carpet, take us today,
To a land that's far, far away
Where ghosts fly through the night and call.
Take us, Magic Carpet, one and all.

Lesson 6, Part 2 Extra! Extra!

Halloween Fun

To the tune of "The Mulberry Bush"

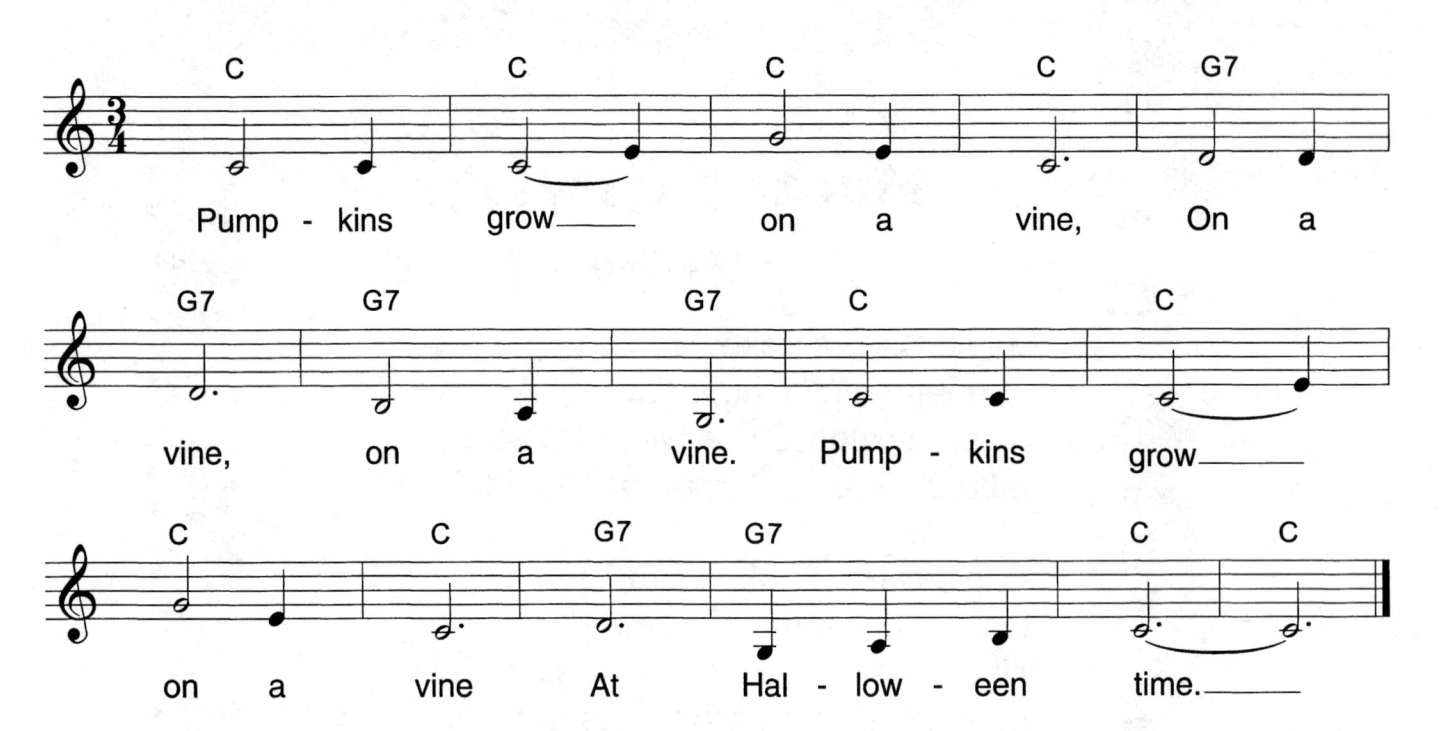

Pump - kins grow on a vine, On a vine, on a vine. Pump - kins grow on a vine At Hal - low - een time.

2. Pumpkins grow orange and round,
   Orange and round, orange and round.
   Pumpkins grow orange and round
   At Halloween time.

3. This is the way we pick the pumpkin,
   Pick the pumpkin, pick the pumpkin.
   This is the way we pick the pumpkin
   At Halloween time.

4. This is the way we scoop the seeds,
   Scoop the seeds, scoop the seeds.
   This is the way we scoop the seeds
   At Halloween time.

5. This is the way we carve a face,
   Carve a face, carve a face.
   This is the way we carve a face
   At Halloween time.

6. We light the candle and let it shine,
   Let it shine, let it shine.
   We light the candle and let it shine
   At Halloween time.

7. We dress in costume and trick-or-treat,
   Trick-or-treat, trick-or-treat.
   We dress in costume and trick-or-treat
   At Halloween time.

Lesson 6, Part 1

Pumpkin, Pumpkin
(poem)

Pumpkin, pumpkin, God made you
(Extend arms in big circle.)

Big and fat and round.
(Shake arms side to side.)

I'm glad you smile on Halloween
(Point to smile.)

And never make a sound.
(Put finger to lips for silence.)

Your face is always cheery,
(Open hands at side of face.)

With mouth and eyes and nose.
(Point to mouth, eyes, nose.)

With a bright and shiny candle
(Put index finger straight up.)

See how my pumpkin glows!
(Open and close hands quickly.)

Discovering God's Love Songbook

Thanksgiving Song

To the tune of "Away in a Manger"

Thanks - giv - ing is com - ing And we will give thanks, Re - mem - b'ring the Pil - grims Who sailed to our banks. They worked and they plant - ed. They wor - shiped and prayed, Re - joic - ing in bless - ings And new friends they'd made.

Lesson 8, Part 1

The Bible

To the tune of "London Bridge"

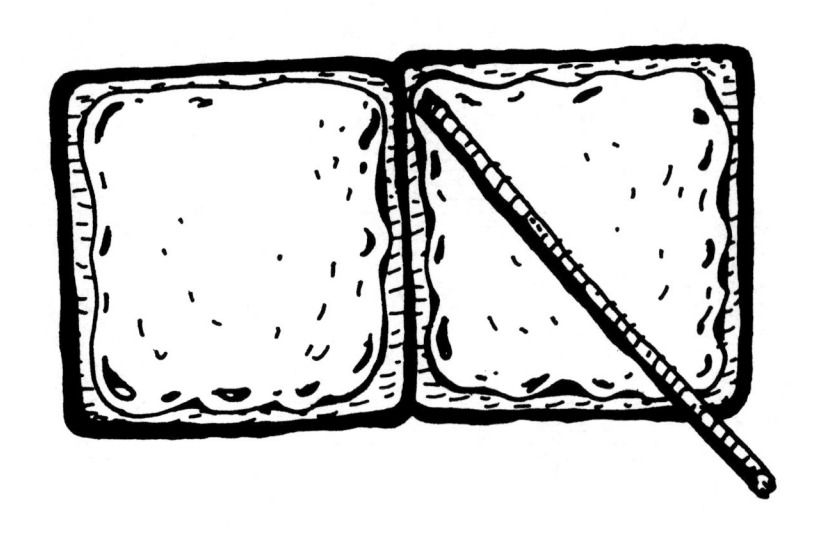

The Bi - ble is God's ho - ly book, God's ho - ly book, God's ho - ly book. The Bi - ble is God's ho - ly book. Let's read a Bi - ble sto - ry.

20 Discovering God's Love Songbook

Winter's Here

To the tune of "Frère Jacques"

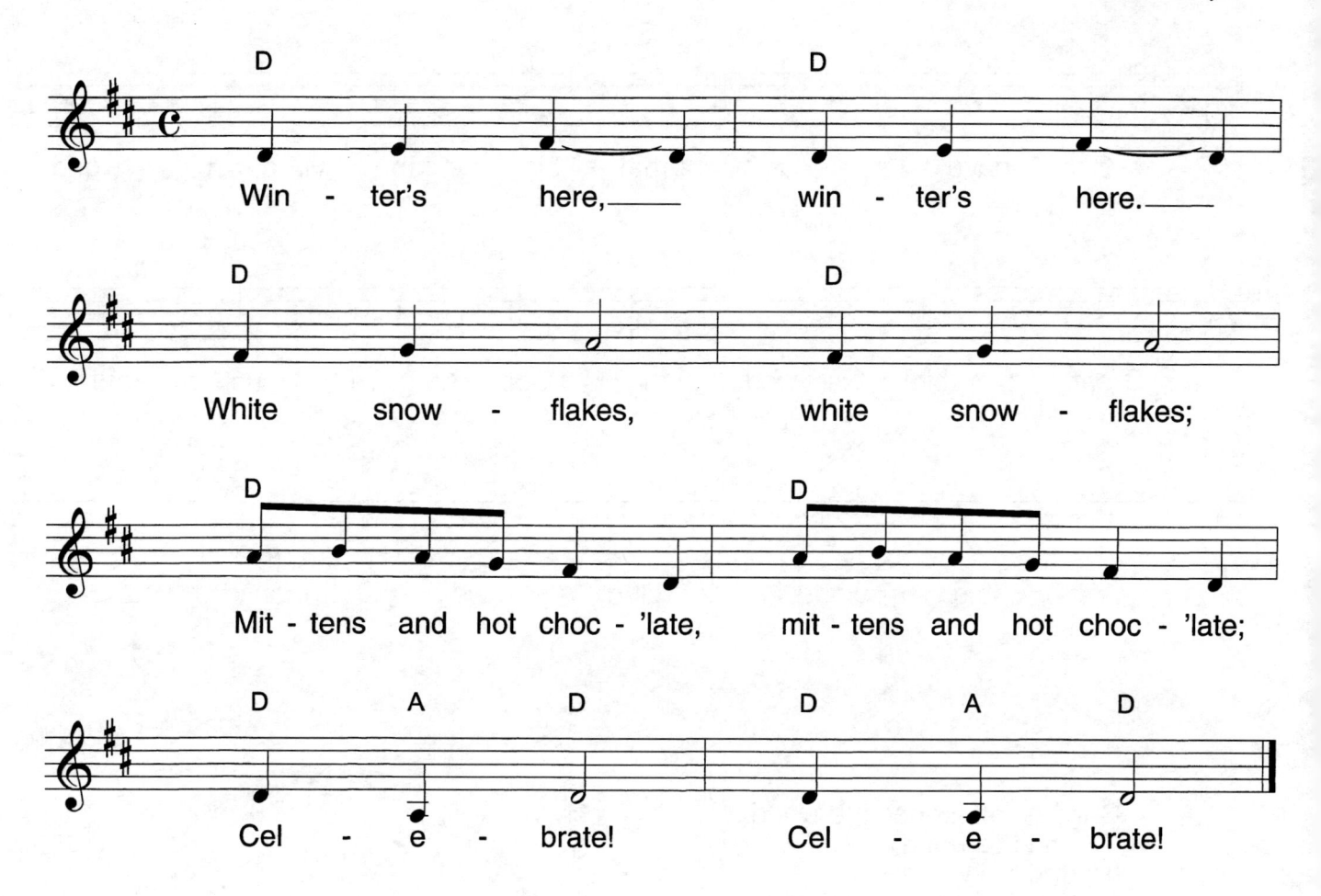

Win - ter's here, win - ter's here.
White snow - flakes, white snow - flakes;
Mit - tens and hot choc - 'late, mit - tens and hot choc - 'late;
Cel - e - brate! Cel - e - brate!

Lesson 9, Part 1

God's Great Big World

To the tune of "London Bridge"

God gave us our great big world, Great big world,

Great big world. God gave us our

great big world. God, we thank you.

2. Children all around the world,
   'Round the world,
   'Round the world,
   Children all around the world:
   God, we thank you.

22 Discovering God's Love Songbook

Lesson 9, Part 3

God Made Everything

To the tune of
"Twinkle, Twinkle, Little Star"

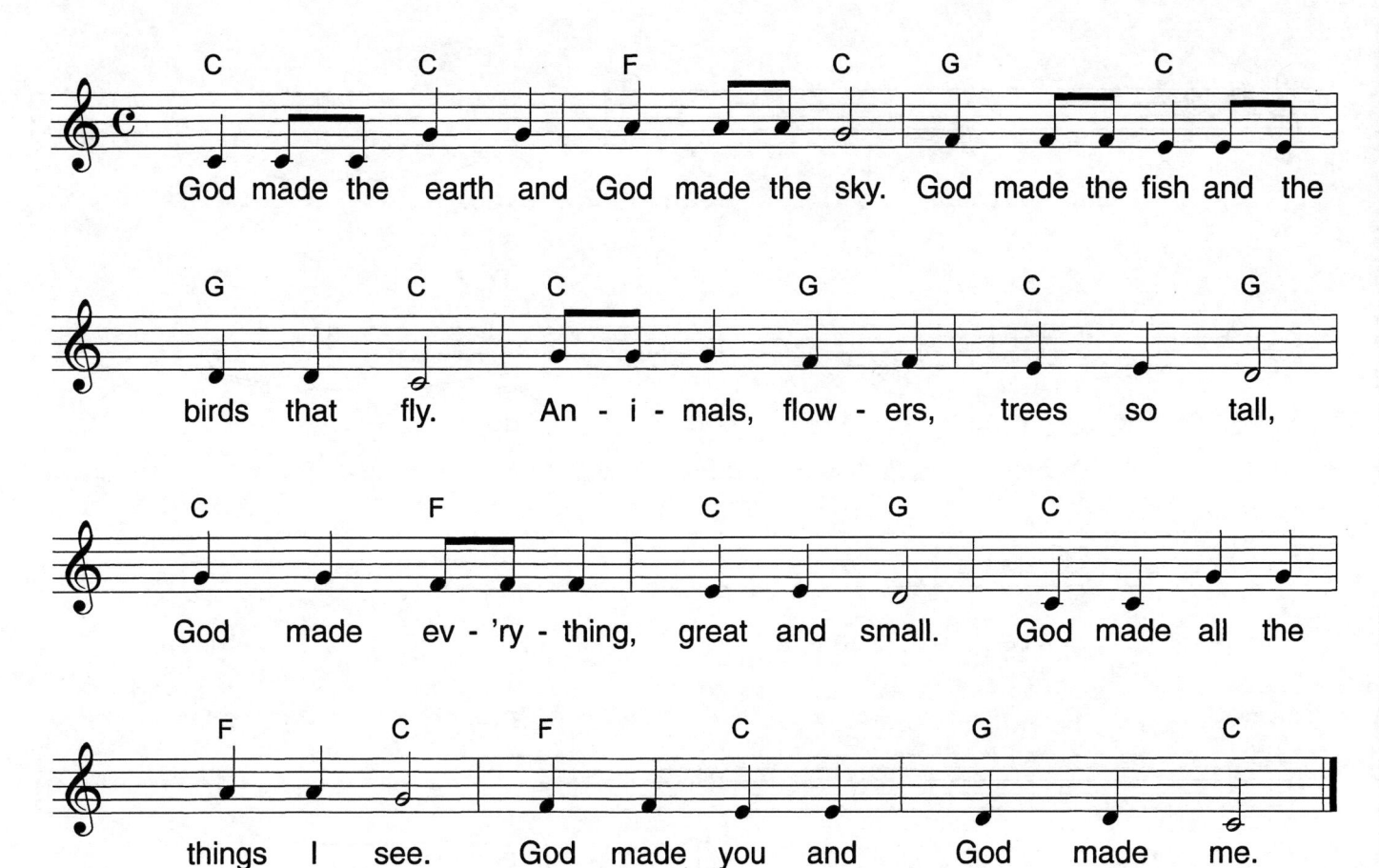

God made the earth and God made the sky. God made the fish and the birds that fly. An-i-mals, flow-ers, trees so tall, God made ev-'ry-thing, great and small. God made all the things I see. God made you and God made me.

Discovering God's Love Songbook **23**

Lesson 10, Part 1

See What I Can Do

*To the tune of
"The Farmer in the Dell"*

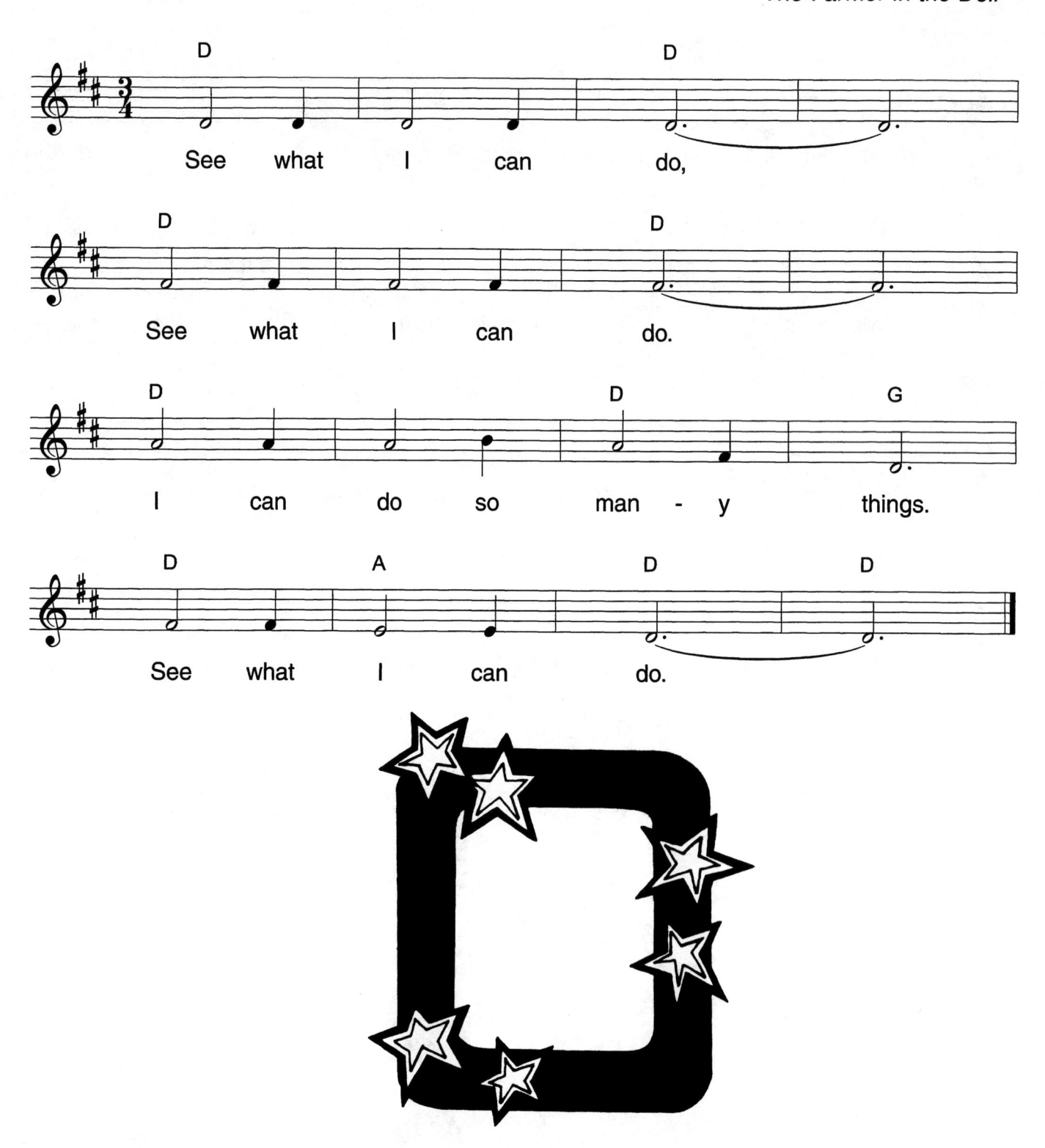

See what I can do,

See what I can do.

I can do so man - y things.

See what I can do.

24 Discovering God's Love Songbook

I Am Special

To the tune of
"If You're Happy and You Know It"

I am spe - cial and I know it, clap my hands. I am spe - cial and I know it, clap my hands. I am spe - cial and I know it, And it's oh such fun to show it. I am spe - cial and I know it, clap my hands.

2. Let me show you all the things that I can do. (tap, tap)
   Let me show you all the things that I can do. (tap, tap)
   I am special and I know it,
   And it's oh such fun to show it.
   Let me show you all the things that I can do. (tap, tap)

Discovering God's Love Songbook

Lesson 11, Part 2 Extra! Extra!

An Activity Song

*To the tune of
"The Mulberry Bush"*

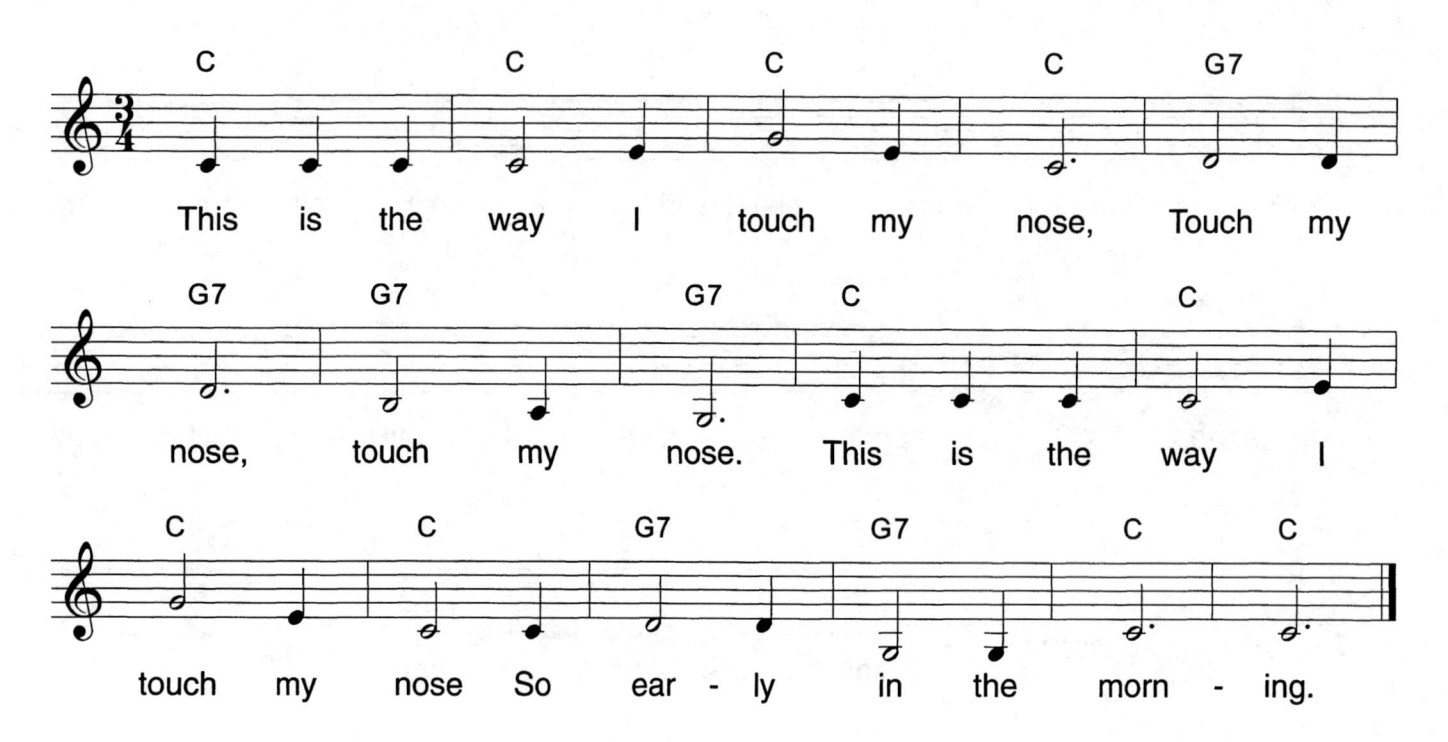

This is the way I touch my nose, Touch my nose, touch my nose. This is the way I touch my nose So ear-ly in the morn-ing.

2. This is the way I open my mouth,
   Open my mouth, open my mouth.
   This is the way I open my mouth
   So early in the morning.

3. This is the way I clap my hands,
   Clap my hands, clap my hands.
   This is the way I clap my hands
   So early in the morning.

26 Discovering God's Love Songbook

4. This is the way I pat my head,
   Pat my head, pat my head.
   This is the way I pat my head
   So early in the morning.

5. This is the way I blink my eyes,
   Blink my eyes, blink my eyes.
   This is the way I blink my eyes
   So early in the morning.

6. This is the way I stamp my left foot,
   Stamp my left foot, stamp my left foot.
   This is the way I stamp my left foot
   So early in the morning.

7. This is the way I hop on one foot,
   Hop on one foot, hop on one foot.
   This is the way I hop on one foot
   So early in the morning.

8. This is the way I touch my toes,
   Touch my toes, touch my toes.
   This is the way I touch my toes
   So early in the morning.

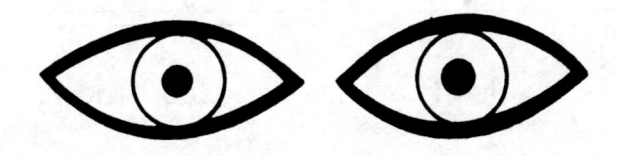

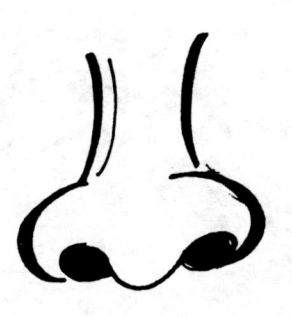

Lesson 11, Part 2

I'm Learning About My God

To the tune of "Go 'Round the Village"

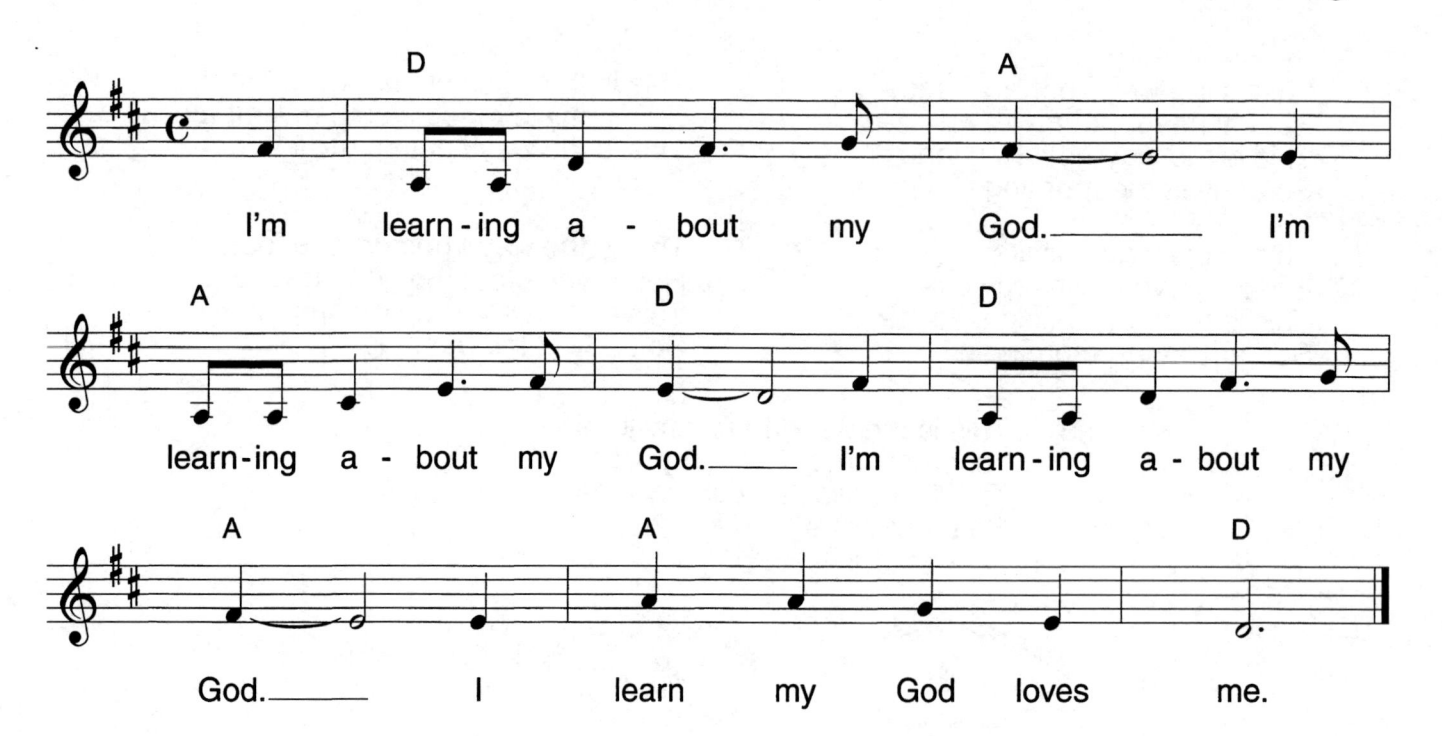

I'm learn-ing a - bout my God. I'm learn-ing a - bout my God. I'm learn-ing a - bout my God. I learn my God loves me.

2. I'm learning about my God.
   I'm learning about my God.
   I'm learning about my God,
   My God who has made me.

3. I'm learning about my God.
   I'm learning about my God.
   I'm learning about my God,
   My God who knows my name.

4. I'm learning about my God.
   I'm learning about my God.
   I'm learning about my God,
   My God who made our world.

28 Discovering God's Love Songbook

I Am Growing (#2)

To the tune of "Mary Had a Little Lamb"

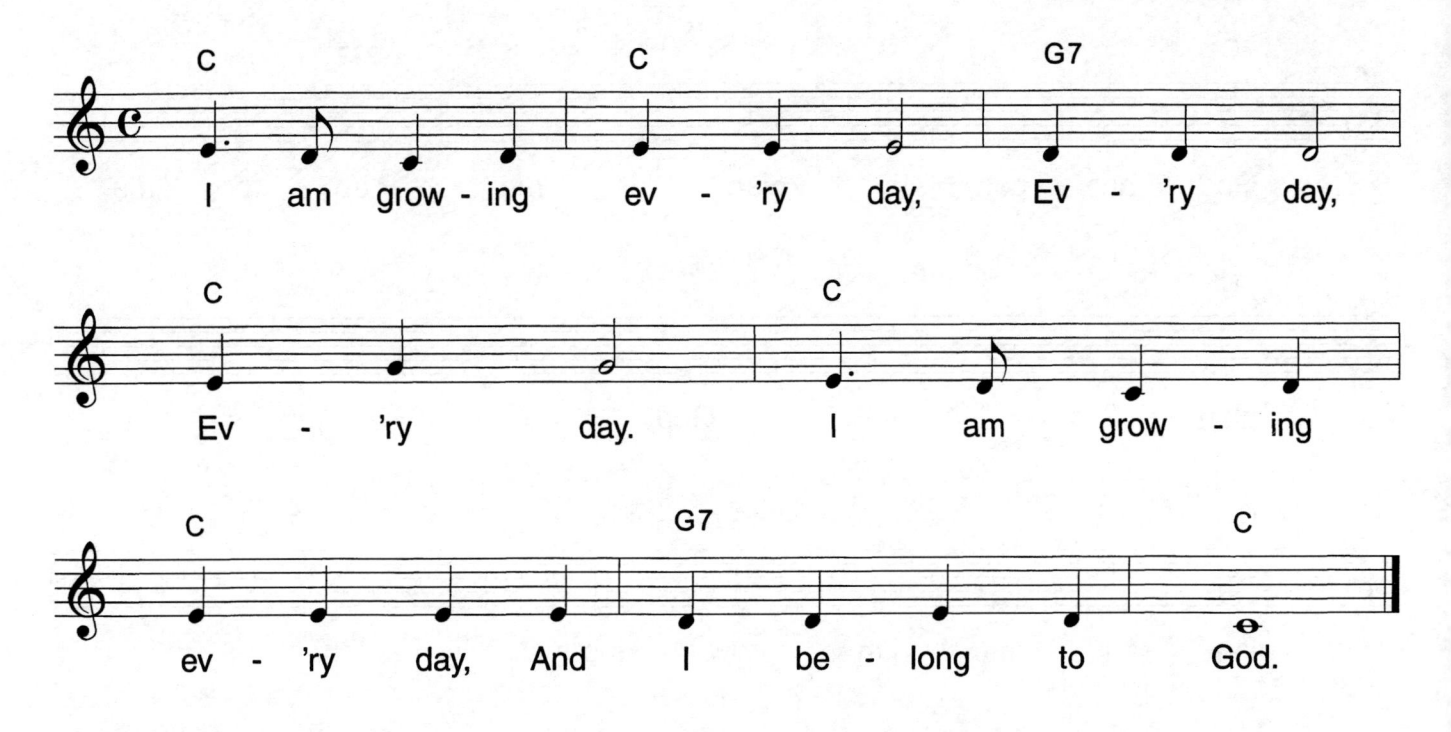

I am grow-ing ev-'ry day, Ev-'ry day, Ev-'ry day. I am grow-ing ev-'ry day, And I be-long to God.

2. I am learning how to live,
   How to live,
   How to live.
   I am learning how to live
   As a child of God.

Discovering God's Love Songbook

Lesson 12, Part 3

God Has a Plan

*To the tune of
"Mary Had a Little Lamb"*

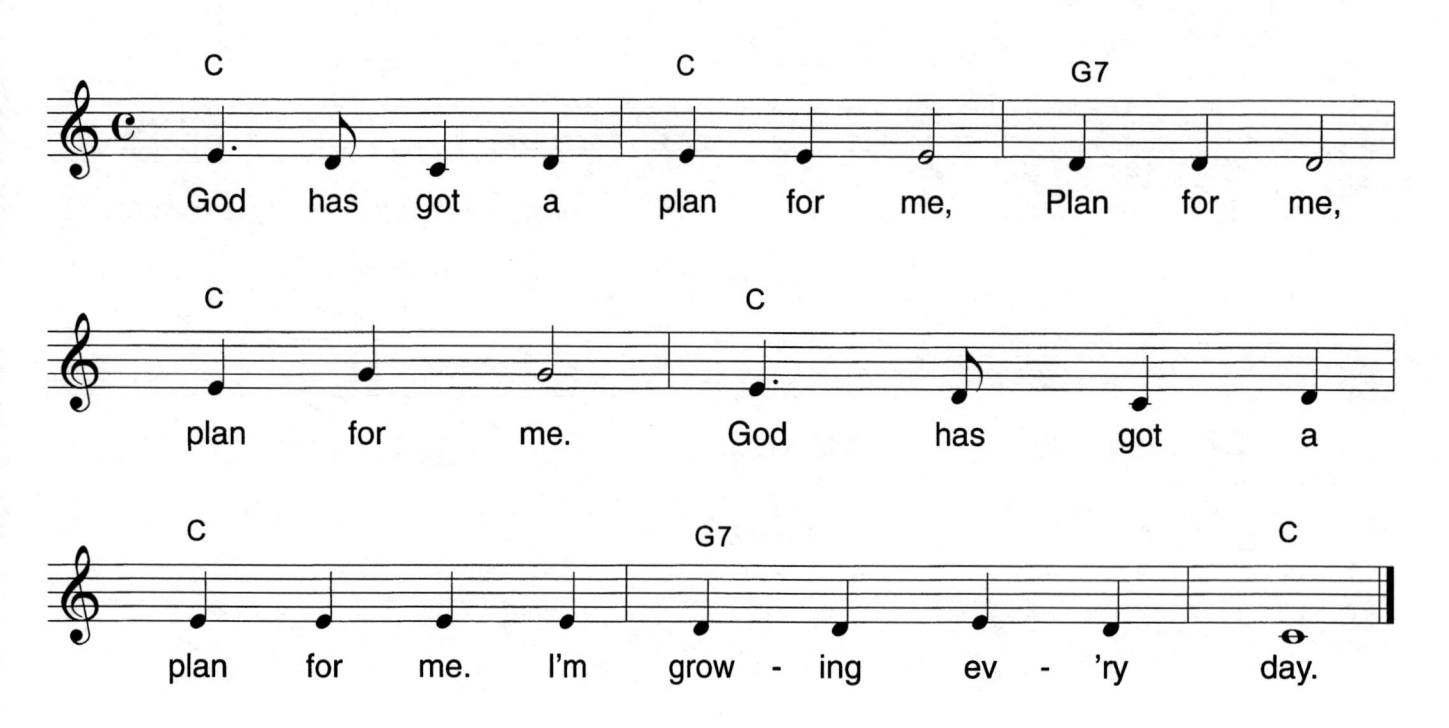

God has got a plan for me, Plan for me,
plan for me. God has got a
plan for me. I'm grow-ing ev-'ry day.

2. I'm growing in my family,
   Family, family.
   I'm growing in my family,
   And in God's fam'ly, too.

I like to fish with Pop.

30   Discovering God's Love Songbook

Lesson 13, Part 2

Feelings

To the tune of
"Sing a Song of Sixpence"

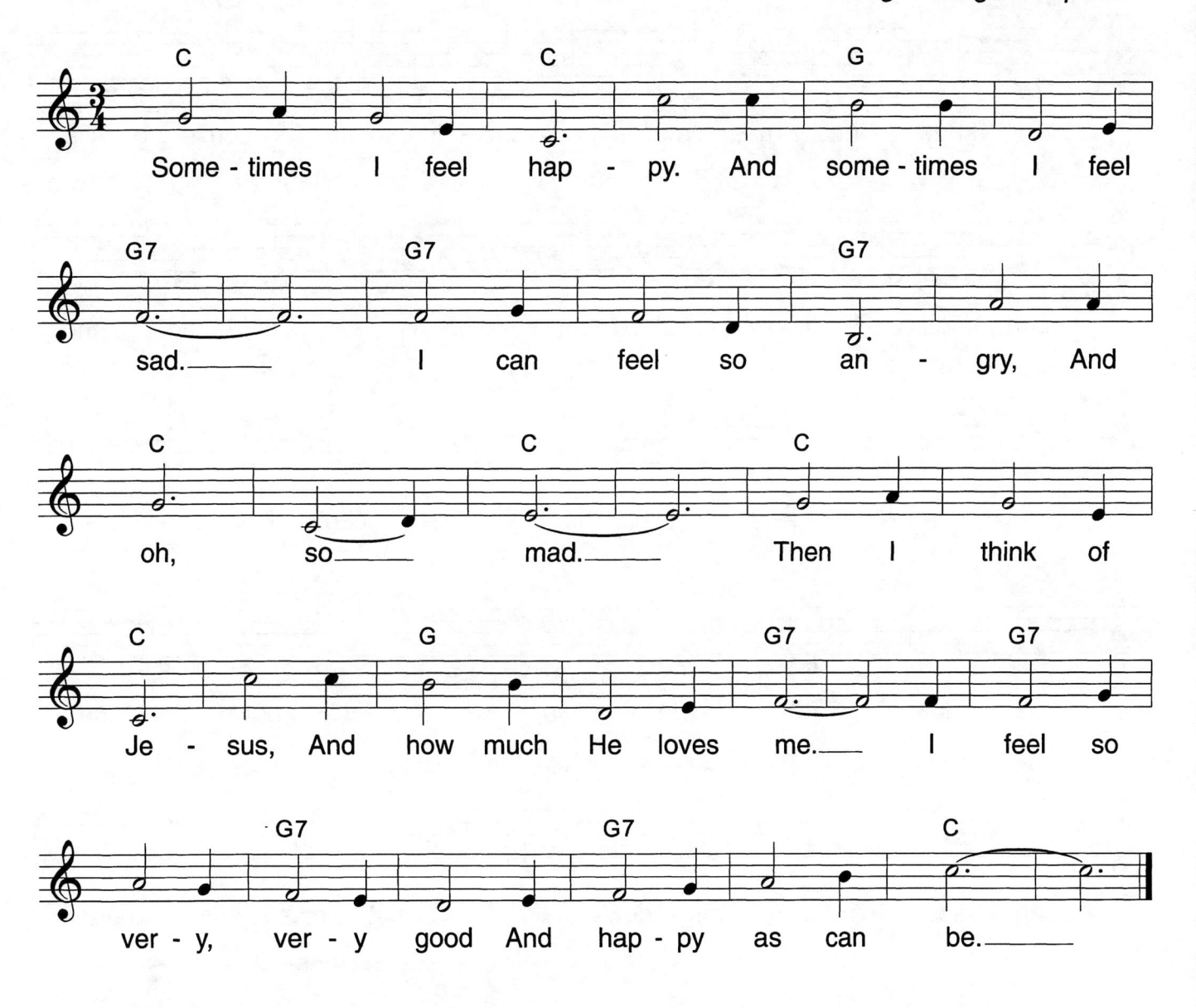

Some-times I feel hap-py. And some-times I feel sad. I can feel so an-gry, And oh, so mad. Then I think of Je-sus, And how much He loves me. I feel so ver-y, ver-y good And hap-py as can be.

2. I think of all the many gifts
   That God has given me.
   I thank you, God, for feelings.
   I need them all you see.
   And I think of Jesus,
   And how much he loves me.
   I feel so very, very good
   And happy as can be!

Discovering God's Love Songbook

Lesson 14, Part 3

Christmas Is Coming

To the tune of "Did You Ever See a Lassie?"

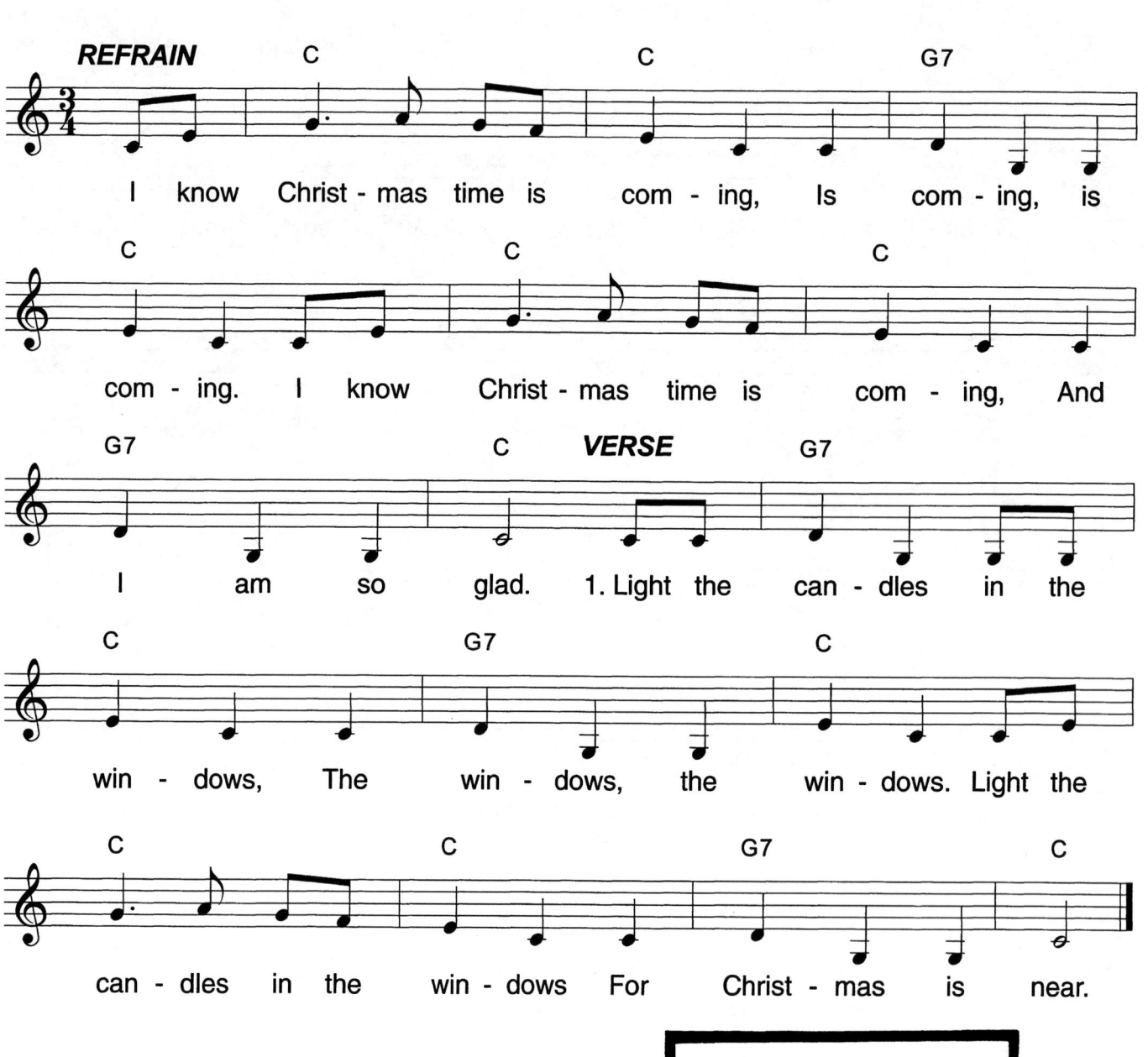

REFRAIN

I know Christ-mas time is com-ing, Is com-ing, is com-ing. I know Christ-mas time is com-ing, And I am so glad.

VERSE

1. Light the can-dles in the win-dows, The win-dows, the win-dows. Light the can-dles in the win-dows For Christ-mas is near.

2. Put the wreath upon the doorway,
   The doorway, the doorway.
   Put the wreath upon the doorway
   For Christmas is near.

32 Discovering God's Love Songbook

Lesson 15, Part 1

Christmas

To the tune of
"The Itsy Bitsy Spider"

The lit-tle ba-by Je-sus Was born on Christ-mas Day. Shep-herds came a-long And knelt down on the hay. Dear Moth-er Mar-y Held the babe that morn, and We know the world was hap-py To hear that Christ was born.

Discovering God's Love Songbook 33

Unit 3
Spring Unit Page

Spring Is Here

To the tune of "Frère Jacques"

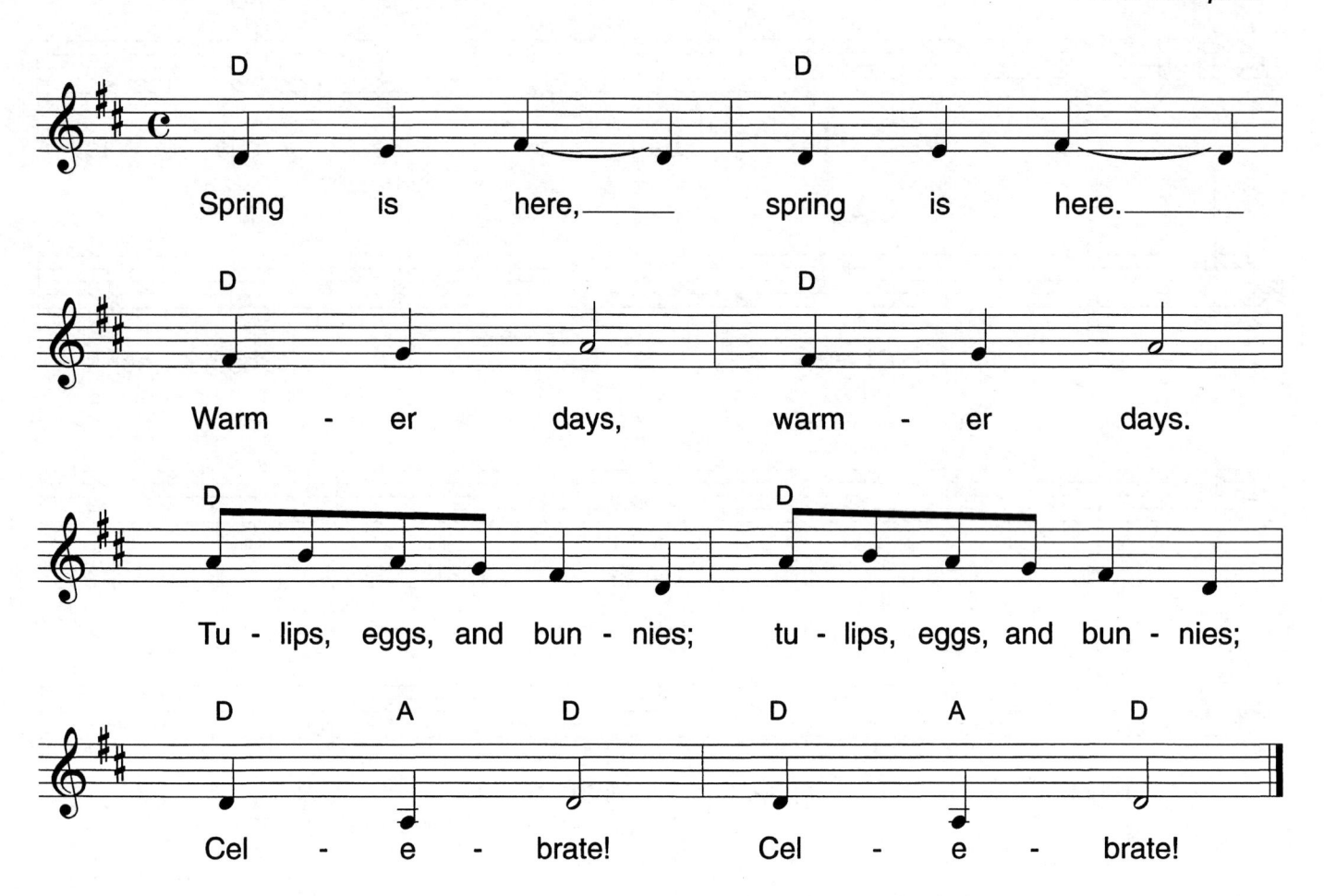

Spring is here, spring is here.

Warm-er days, warm-er days.

Tu-lips, eggs, and bun-nies; tu-lips, eggs, and bun-nies;

Cel-e-brate! Cel-e-brate!

Discovering God's Love Songbook

God Gave Me My Family

To the tune of "London Bridge"

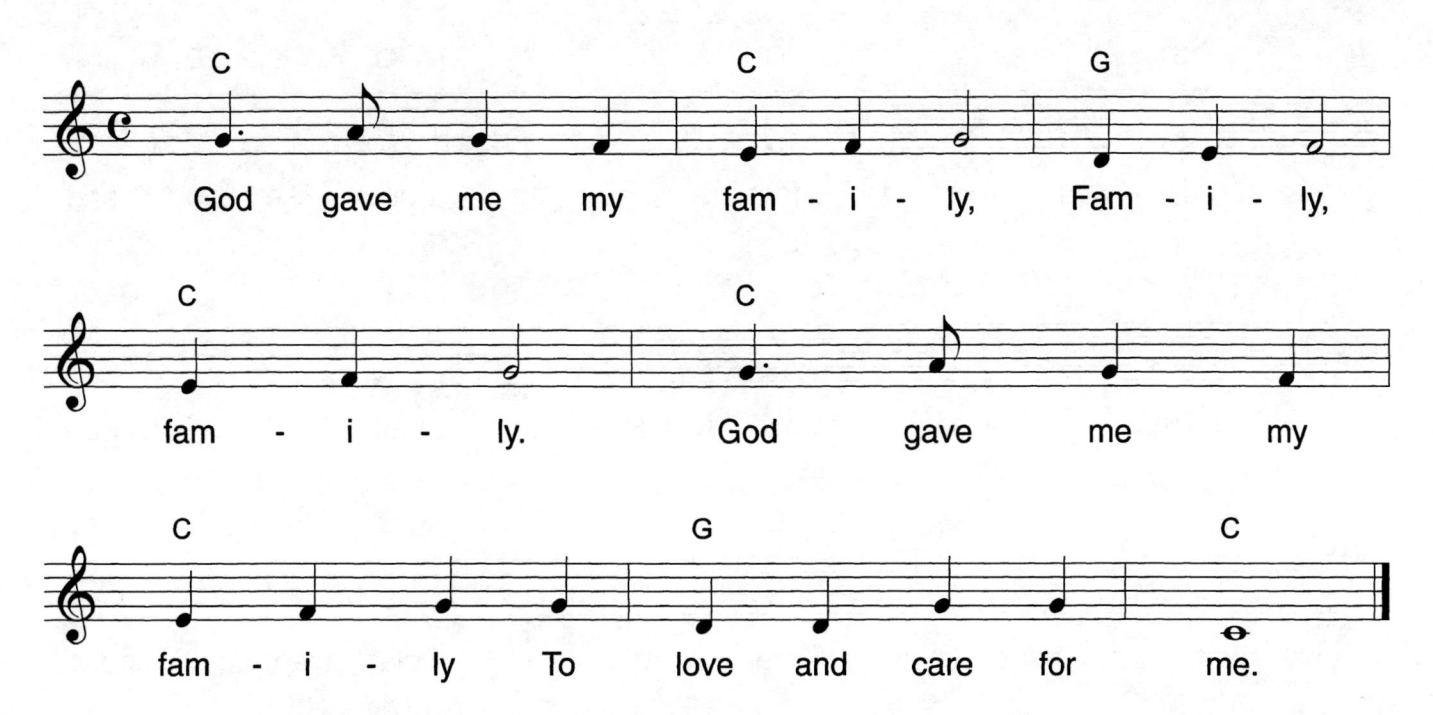

God gave me my fam-i-ly, Fam-i-ly, fam-i-ly. God gave me my fam-i-ly To love and care for me.

2. My fam'ly loves and cares for me,
   Cares for me, cares for me.
   My fam'ly loves and cares for me,
   And I say, "Thank you, God!"

Discovering God's Love Songbook

Lesson 17, Part 3

The Holy Family

To the tune of "Old MacDonald"

Je-sus had a fam-i-ly Just like you and me. His fam-'ly loved him oh so much, Just like mine loves me. With a clap, clap, here, And a clap, clap, there, Here a clap, There a clap, Ev-'ry-where a clap, clap. Je-sus had a fam-i-ly Just like you and me.

Prayer to the Holy Family
Jesus, Mary, and Joseph, too,
I pray to you this day.
Bless my family,
Keep them safe,
In each and every way.

Discovering God's Love Songbook

Helping
(fingerplay)

Five little children
(Hold up hand with five fingers.)
In a family,

Working, playing, singing,
(Shake hands about.)
Happy as can be.

This one is helping
(Raise thumb.)
Mother (Father) care for me.

This one is sharing
(Raise pointer.)
And taking turns you see.

This one is talking
(Raise middle finger.)
In a loving way.

This one is helping
(Raise ring finger.)
Put the toys away.

This last one is happy.
(Raise pinky.)
It's so much fun to share.

Children in a family
(Clasp hands together.)
Show us all they care.

Lesson 19, Part 1

Showing Love

To the tune of "Old MacDonald"

God gave me a fam - i - ly. God is good to me. We work and share, And laugh and play, In my fam - i - ly! With a big hug here, And a big hug there, Here a hug, There a hug, Ev - 'ry - where a hug, hug. God gave me a fam - i - ly. God is good to me.

Discovering God's Love Songbook 39

Lesson 20, Part 1

My Family

To the tune of "Pop Goes the Weasel"

Hap - py, hap - py, hap - py am I, For God gave me a fam - 'ly. We work, we play, and we share a lot. Hoo - ray for my fam - 'ly! Our days are ver - y bus - y, We all have lots to do. But we still love and care a lot. Hoo - ray for my fam - 'ly!

40 Discovering God's Love Songbook

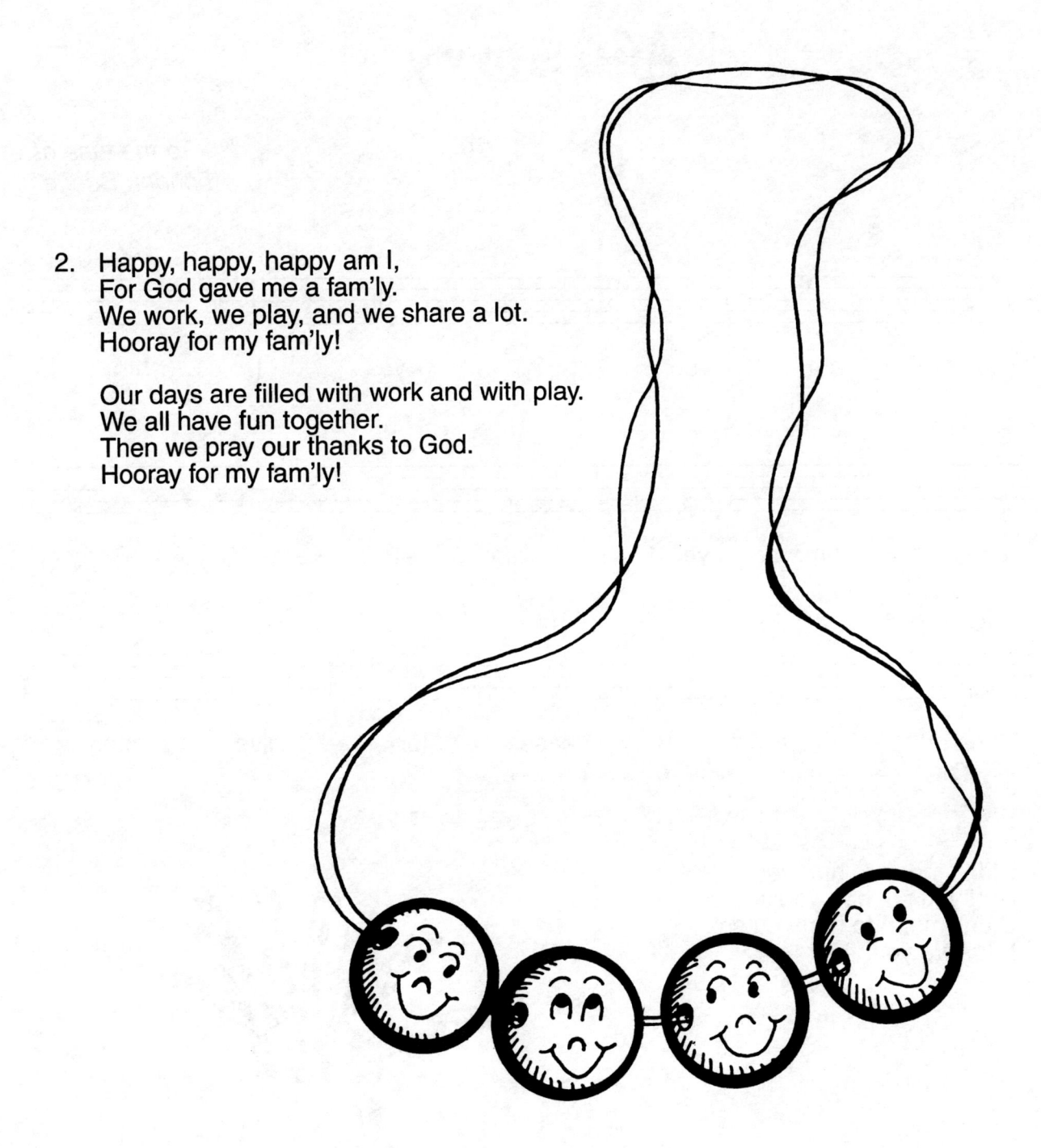

2. Happy, happy, happy am I,
   For God gave me a fam'ly.
   We work, we play, and we share a lot.
   Hooray for my fam'ly!

   Our days are filled with work and with play.
   We all have fun together.
   Then we pray our thanks to God.
   Hooray for my fam'ly!

Discovering God's Love Songbook

I Am Sorry

To the tune of "London Bridge"

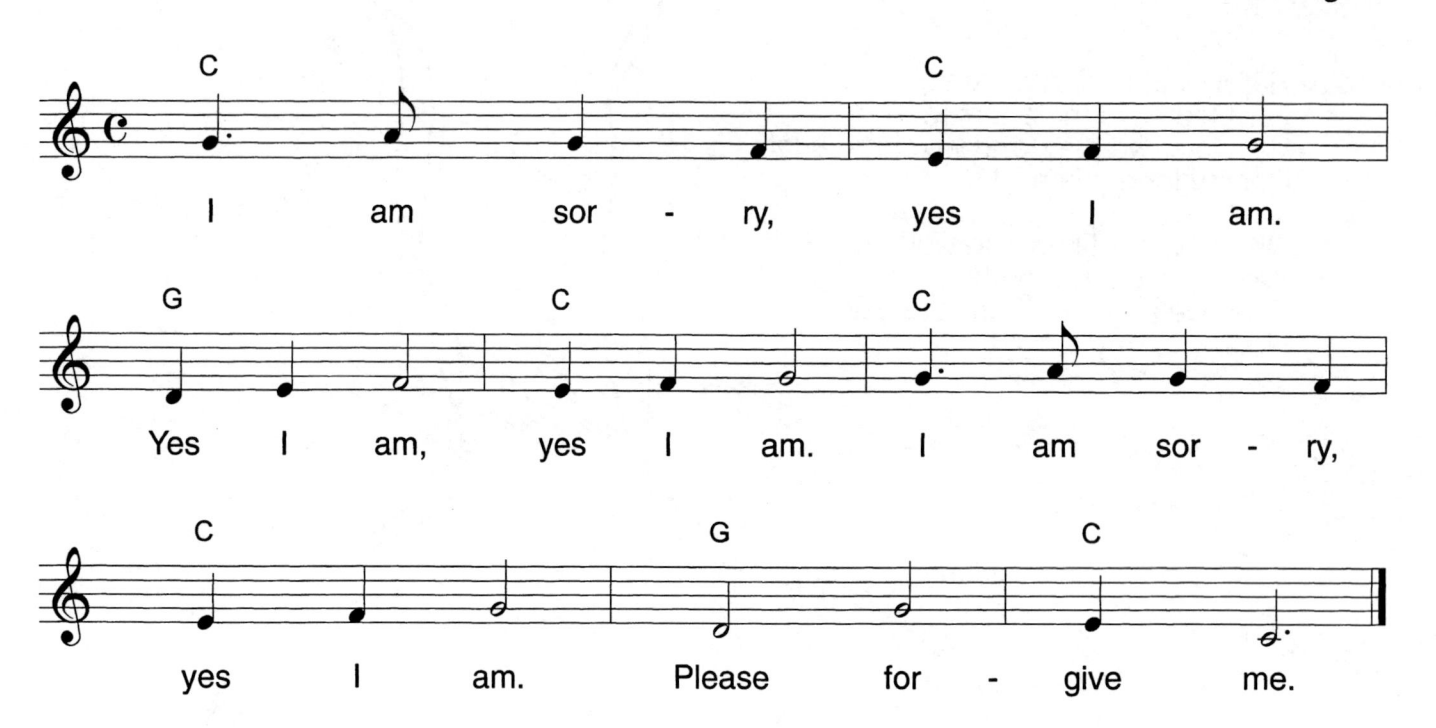

I am sor - ry, yes I am.
Yes I am, yes I am. I am sor - ry,
yes I am. Please for - give me.

2. Didn't mean to hurt you so,
   Hurt you so, hurt you so.
   Didn't mean to hurt you so.
   I do love you.

Lesson 22, Part 1

Valentine's Day

To the tune of "Here We Go Looby-Loo"

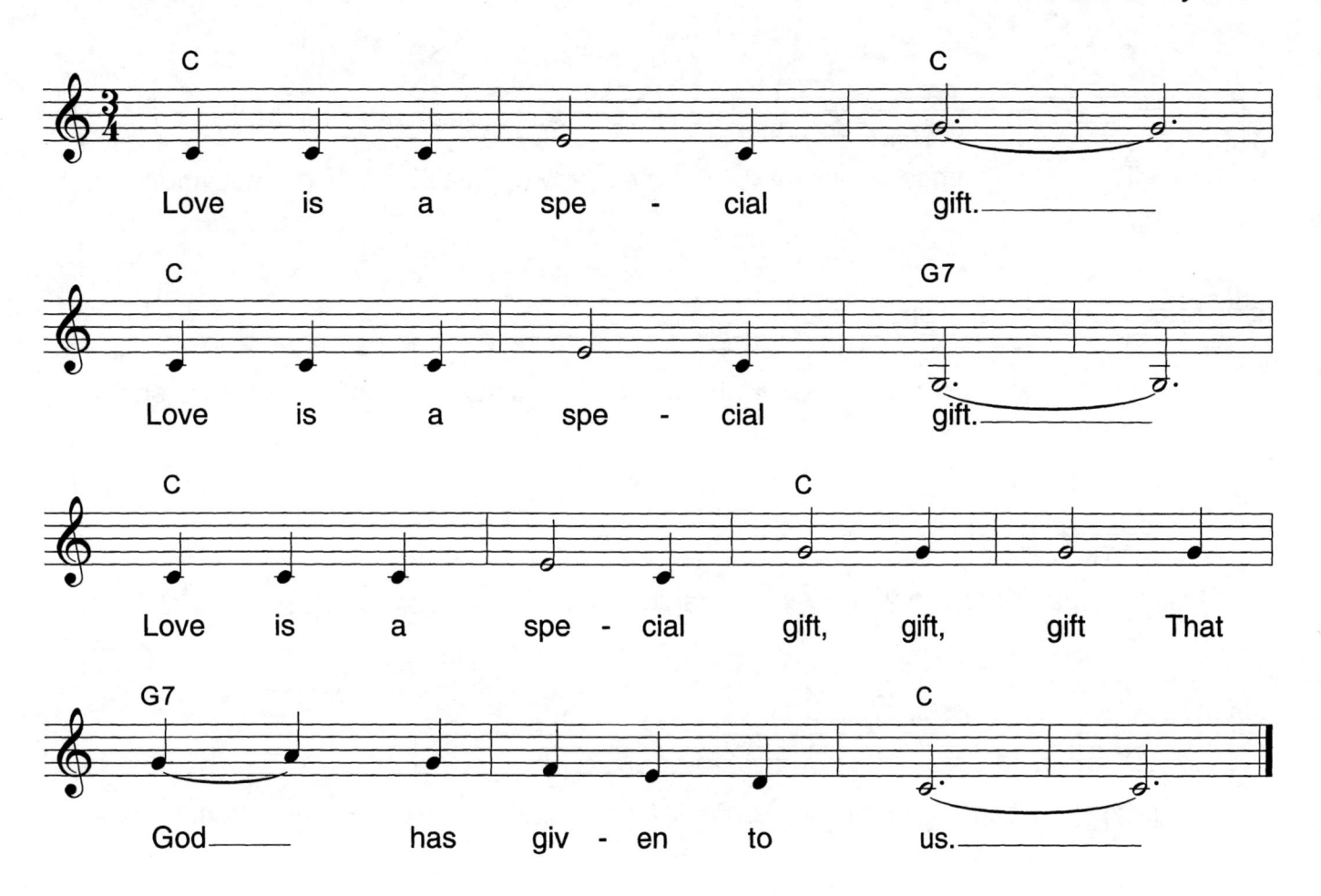

Love is a spe - cial gift.

Love is a spe - cial gift.

Love is a spe - cial gift, gift, gift That

God has giv - en to us.

2. Love makes us want to dance.
   Love makes us want to sing.
   Love fills our hearts with joy, joy, joy.
   God has been so good to us.

Discovering God's Love Songbook 43

Lesson 23, Part 1

Eggs in a Nest

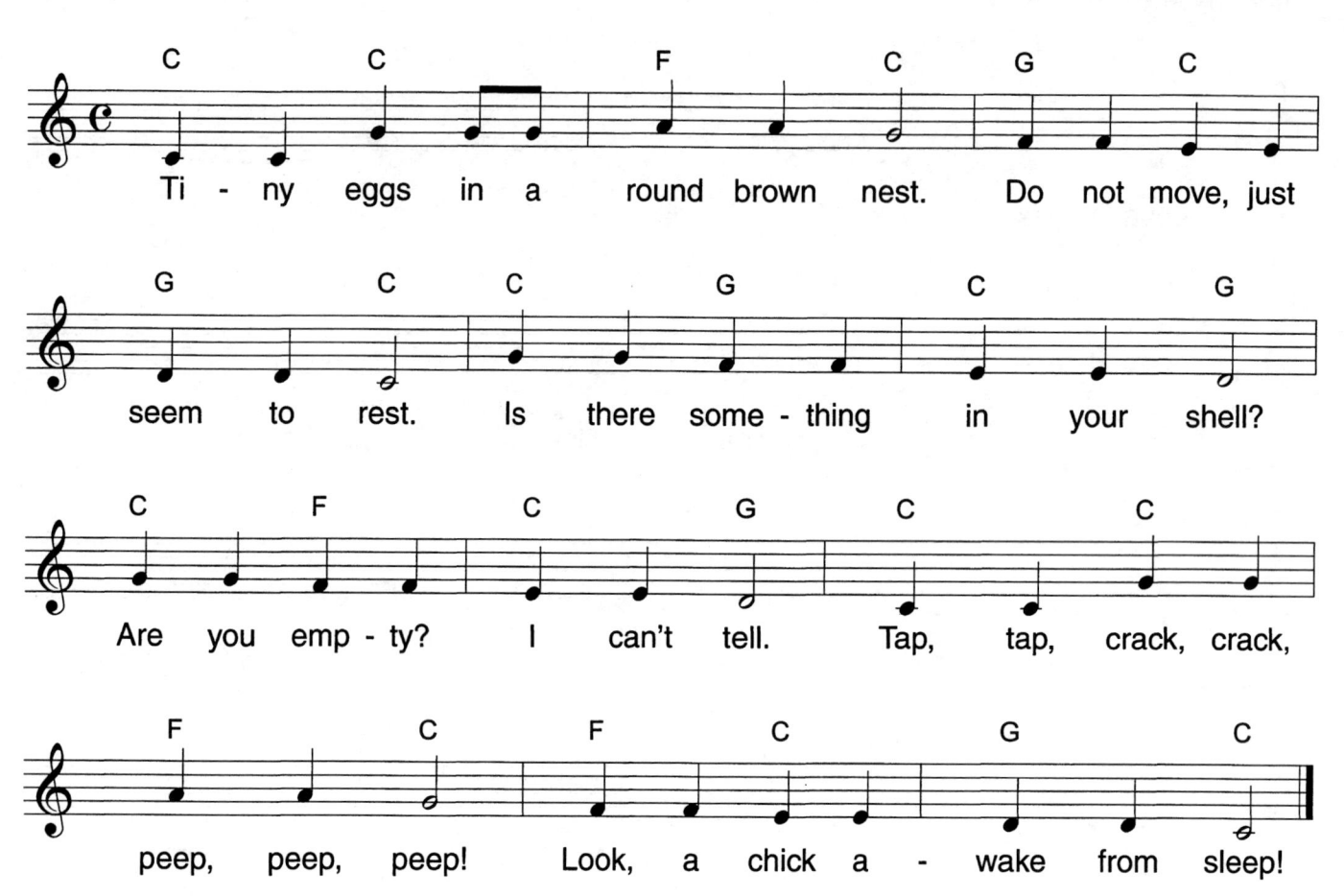

To the tune of
"Twinkle, Twinkle, Little Star"

Ti - ny eggs in a round brown nest. Do not move, just seem to rest. Is there some - thing in your shell? Are you emp - ty? I can't tell. Tap, tap, crack, crack, peep, peep, peep! Look, a chick a - wake from sleep!

44 Discovering God's Love Songbook

Creeping Crawling Caterpillar

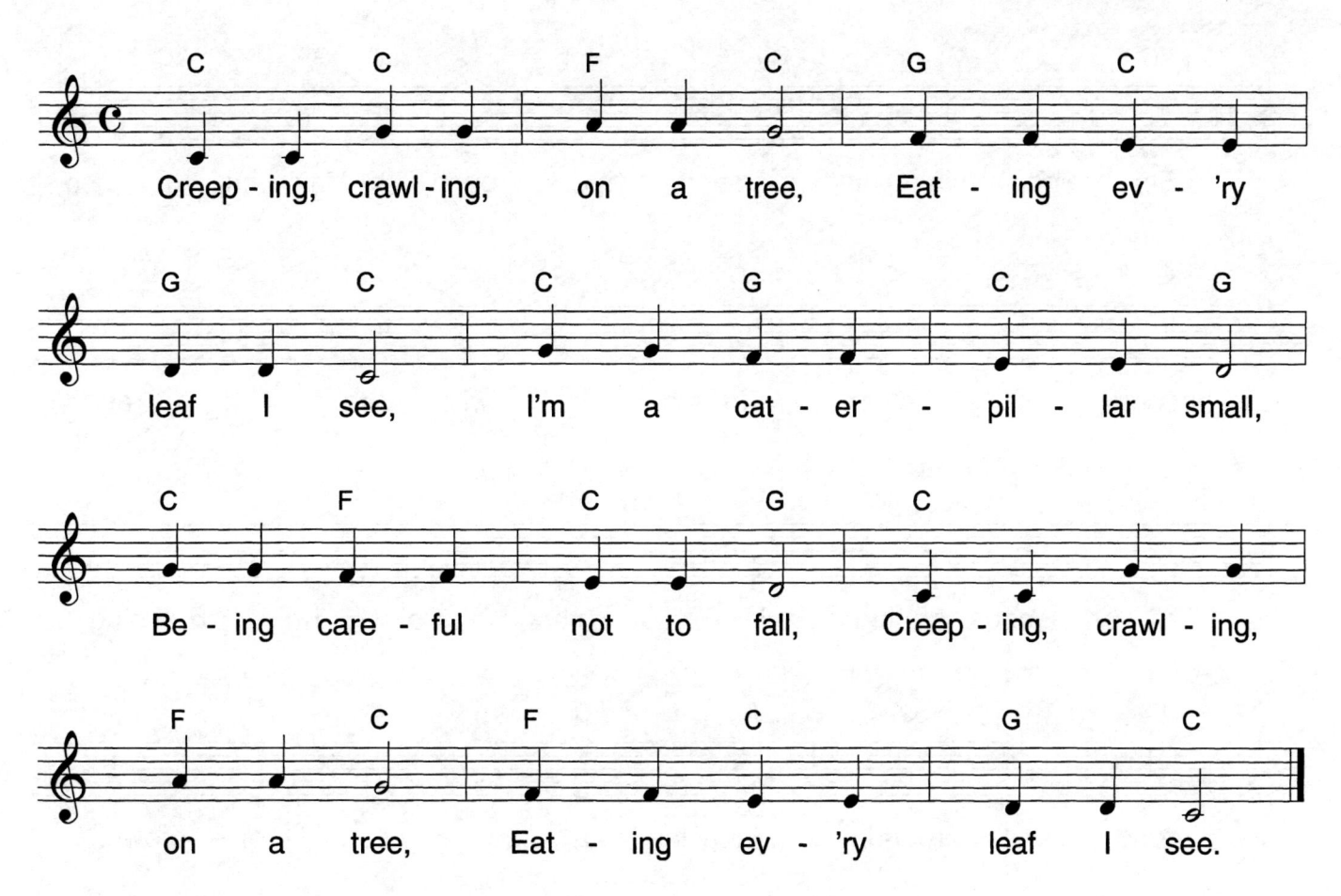

To the tune of
"Twinkle, Twinkle, Little Star"

Creep - ing, crawl - ing, on a tree, Eat - ing ev - 'ry leaf I see, I'm a cat - er - pil - lar small, Be - ing care - ful not to fall, Creep - ing, crawl - ing, on a tree, Eat - ing ev - 'ry leaf I see.

Spinning a Cocoon

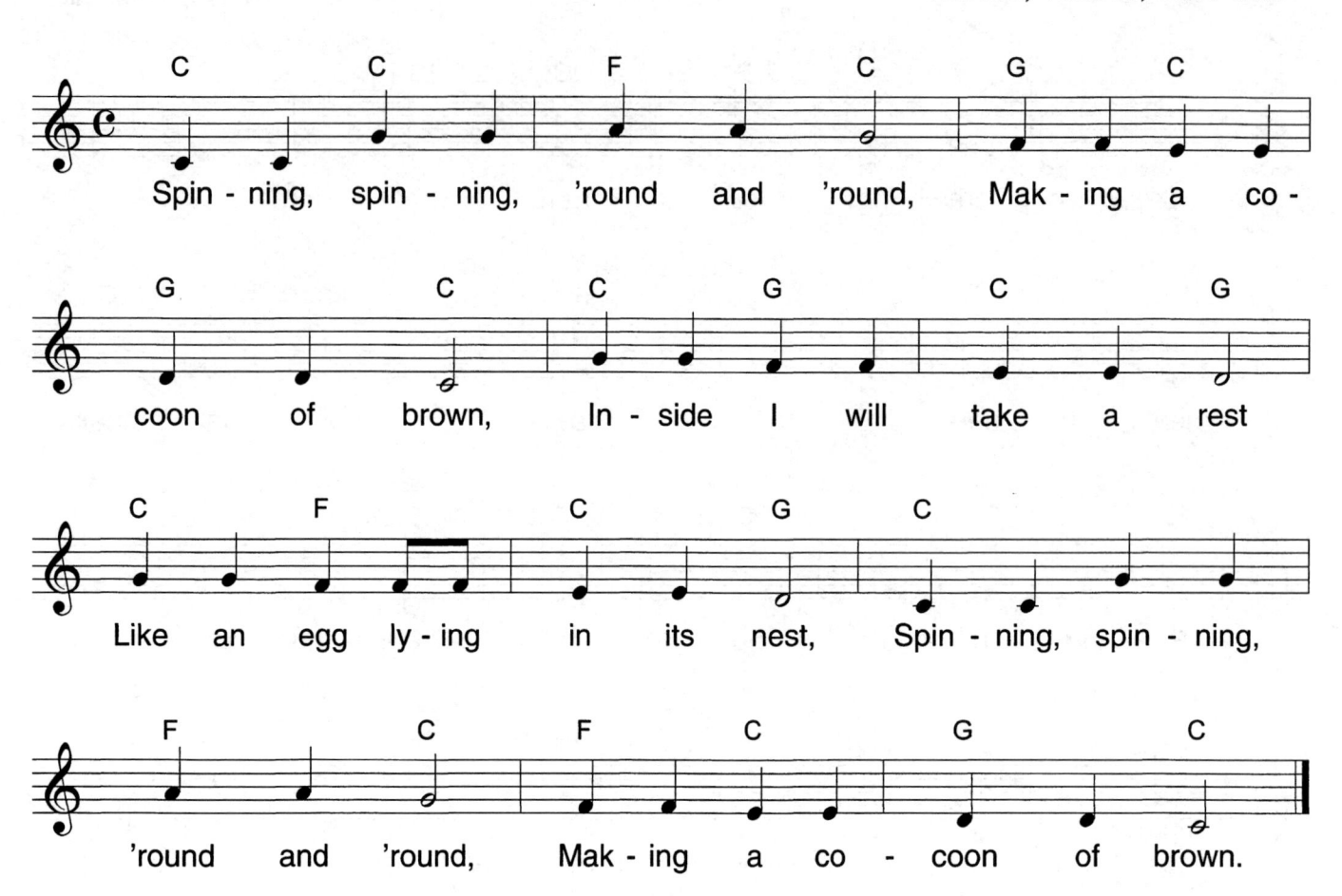

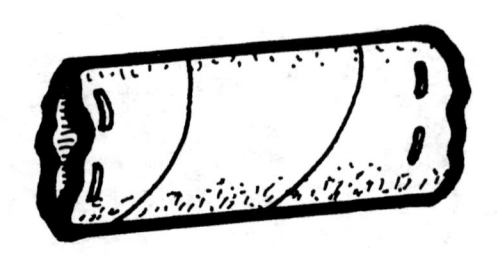

To the tune of
"Twinkle, Twinkle, Little Star"

Spin - ning, spin - ning, 'round and 'round, Mak - ing a co - coon of brown, In - side I will take a rest Like an egg ly - ing in its nest, Spin - ning, spin - ning, 'round and 'round, Mak - ing a co - coon of brown.

Lesson 23, Part 2 Extra! Extra!

Easter

To the tune of "Frère Jacques"

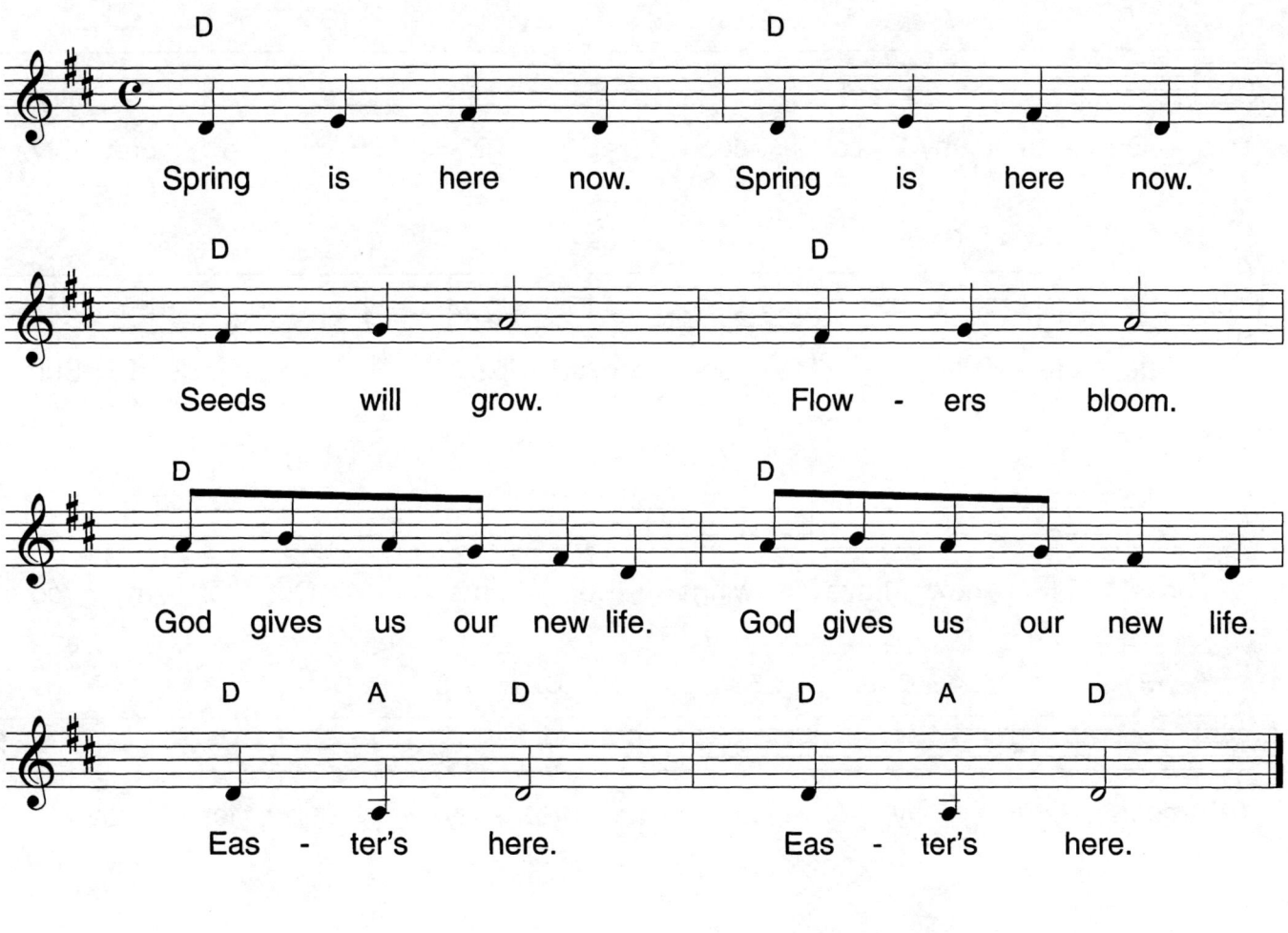

Spring is here now. Spring is here now.
Seeds will grow. Flow-ers bloom.
God gives us our new life. God gives us our new life.
Eas-ter's here. Eas-ter's here.

2. Alleluia!
Alleluia!
Celebrate!
Celebrate!
Jesus Christ is risen.
Jesus Christ is risen.
Easter joy!
Easter joy!

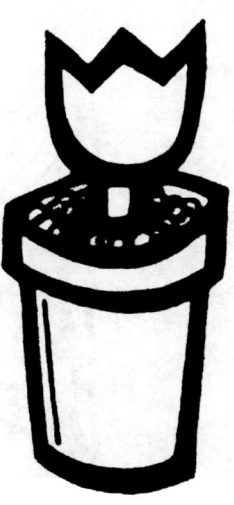

Discovering God's Love Songbook

Pretty Butterfly

*To the tune of
"Twinkle, Twinkle, Little Star"*

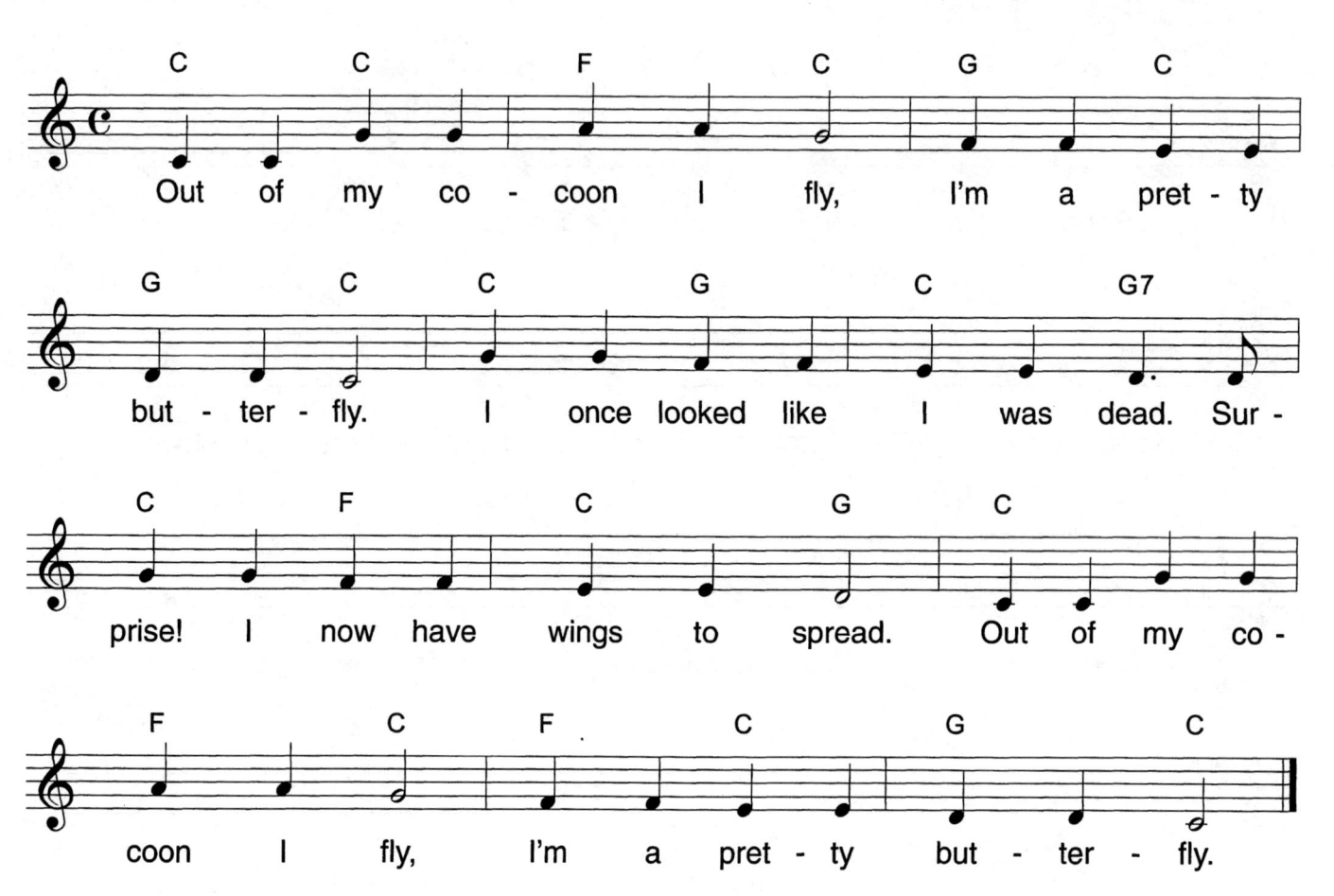

Out of my co-coon I fly, I'm a pret-ty but-ter-fly. I once looked like I was dead. Sur-prise! I now have wings to spread. Out of my co-coon I fly, I'm a pret-ty but-ter-fly.

Let It Shine

*To the tune of
"Mary Had a Little Lamb"*

Hide it un - der a bush - el? No! A bush - el? No! A bush - el? No! Hide it un - der a bush - el? No! Let it shine, let it shine.

Discovering God's Love Songbook

Unit 4
Summer Unit Page

Summer's Coming

To the tune of "Frère Jacques"

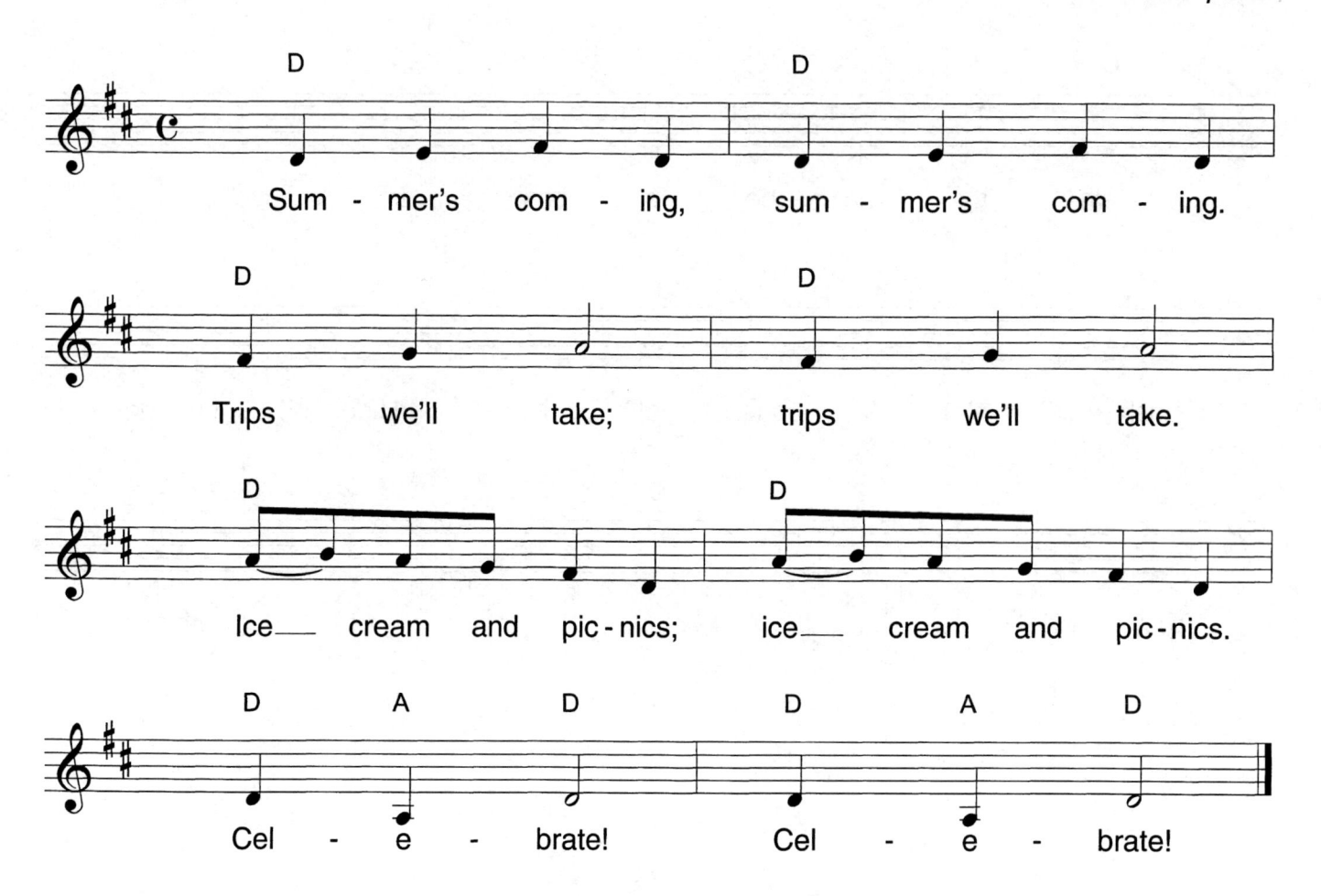

Sum - mer's com - ing, sum - mer's com - ing.

Trips we'll take; trips we'll take.

Ice cream and pic - nics; ice cream and pic - nics.

Cel - e - brate! Cel - e - brate!

50 *Discovering God's Love Songbook*

Lesson 25, Part 2

My Baptism

To the tune of "Mary Had a Little Lamb"

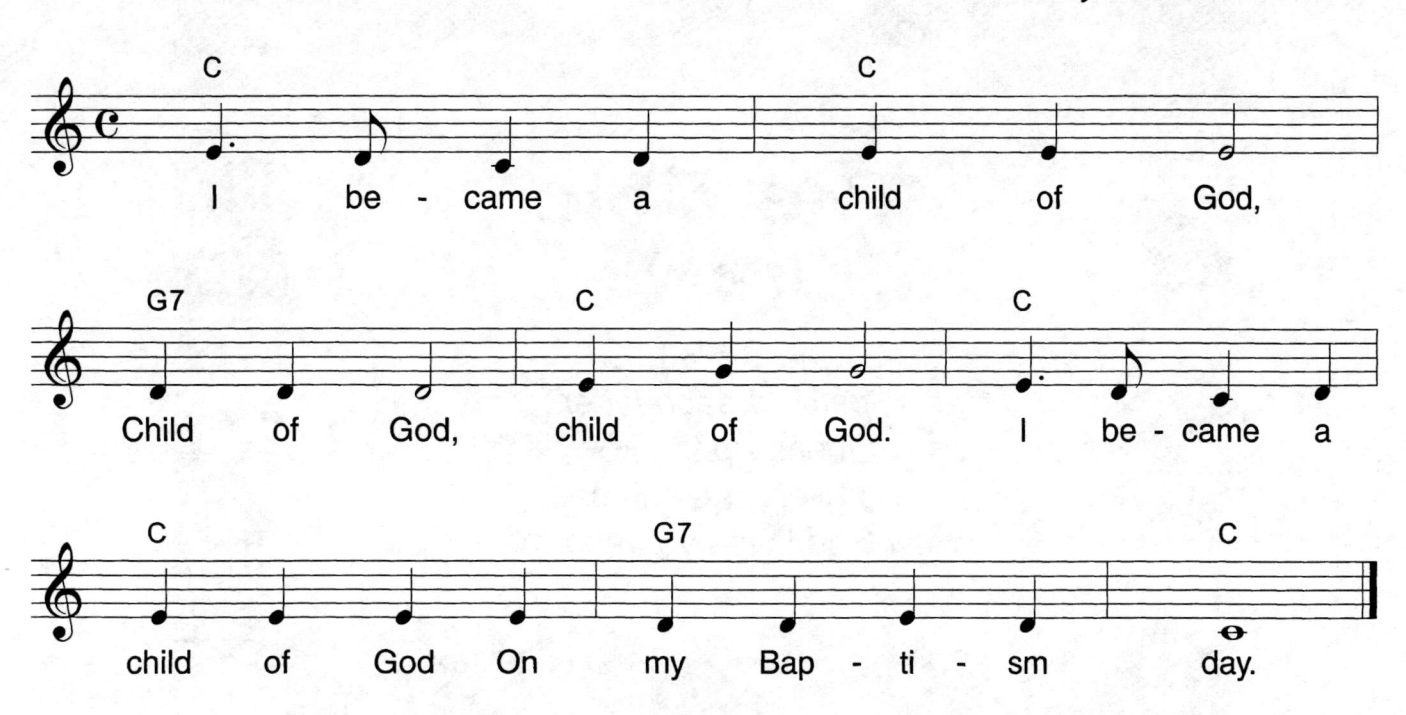

I be-came a child of God,
Child of God, child of God. I be-came a
child of God On my Bap-ti-sm day.

2. Jesus said, "Come, follow me,
   Follow me, follow me."
   Jesus said, "Come, follow me"
   On my Baptism day.

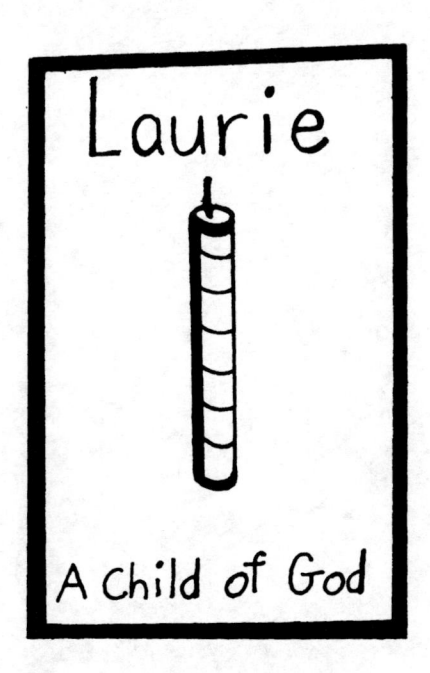

Laurie

A Child of God

Discovering God's Love Songbook 51

Lesson 26, Part 2

The Bible
(poem)

The B-I-B-L-E
(*Spell out each letter.*)
Opens up the key,
So everyone can see
How God loves you and me.

I'm Learning How to Pray

To the tune of "Go 'Round the Village"

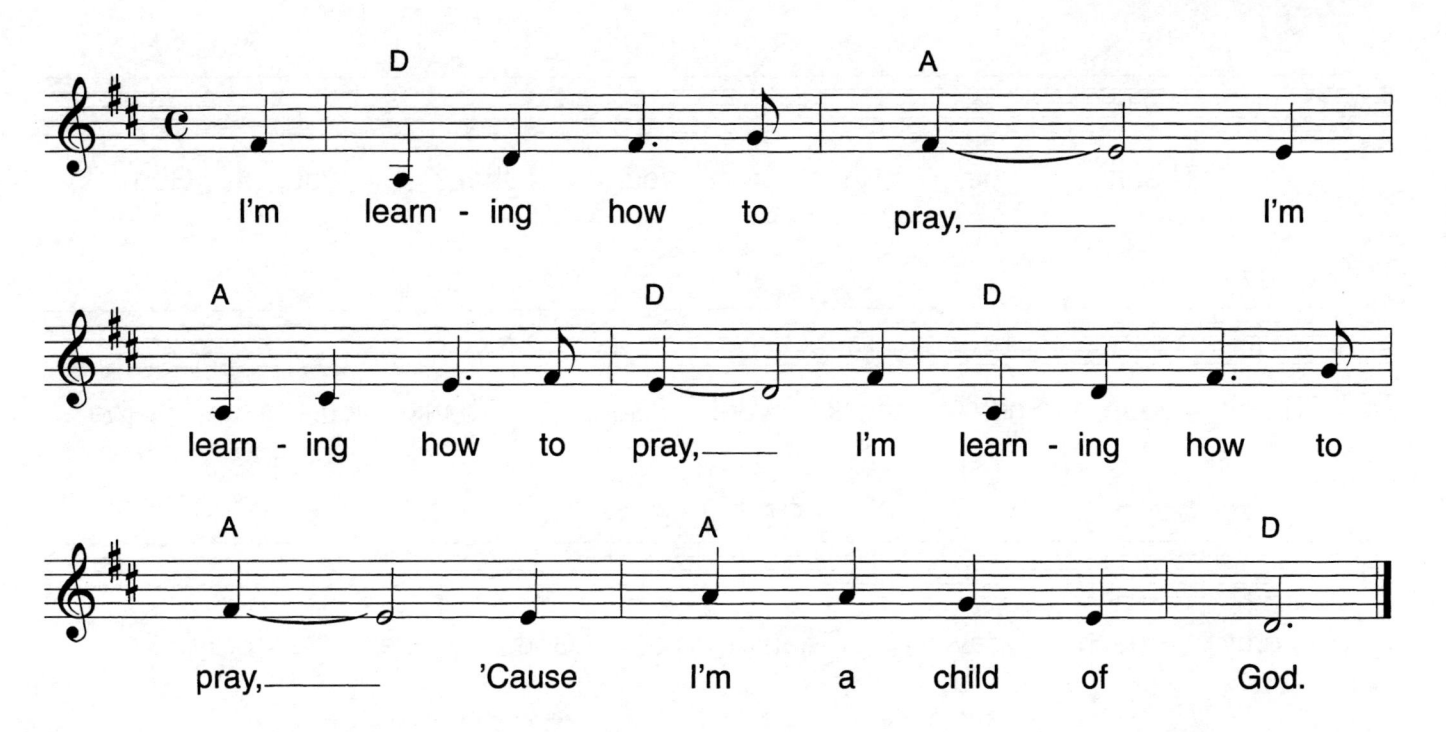

I'm learn-ing how to pray,— I'm learn-ing how to pray,— I'm learn-ing how to pray,— 'Cause I'm a child of God.

2. Jesus taught me how to pray,
   He taught me how to pray,
   Yes, he taught me how to pray,
   'Cause I'm a child of God.

Lesson 27, Part 1

Lesson 27, Part 3

We Pray to God

To the tune of "Mary Had a Little Lamb"

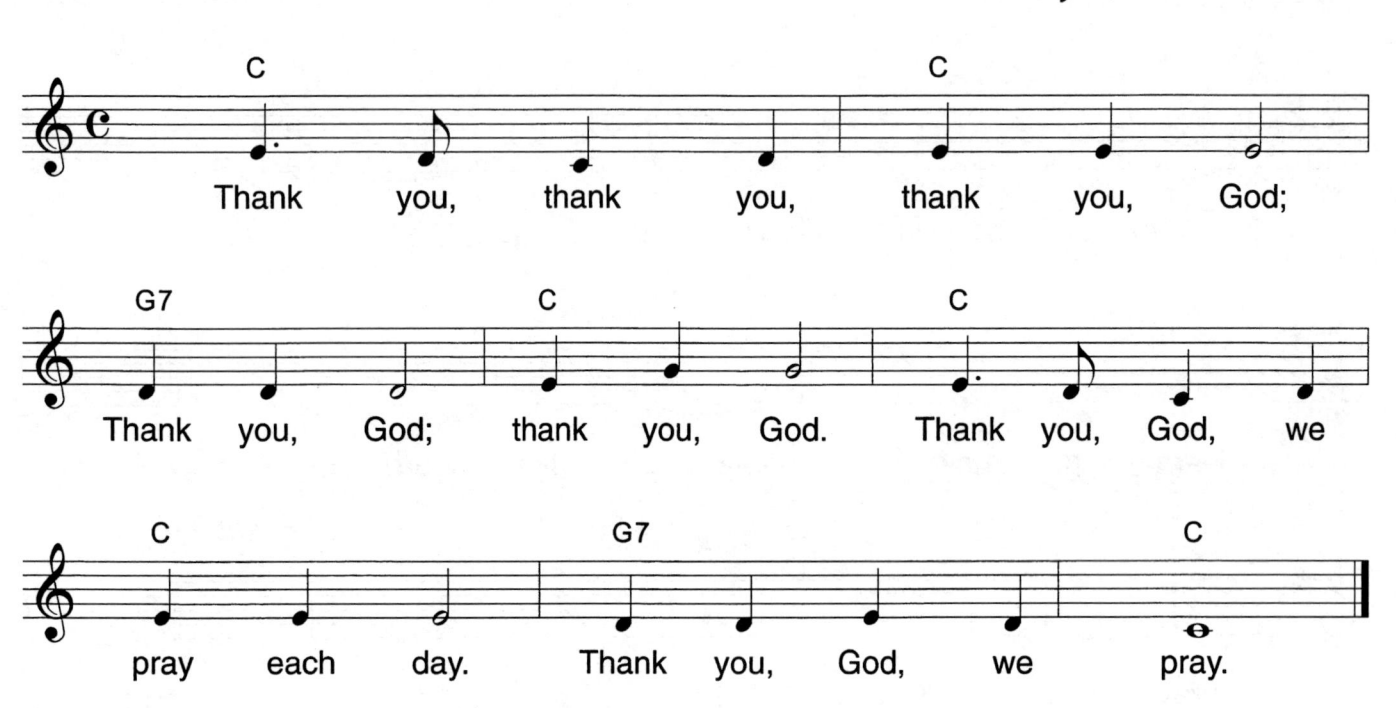

Thank you, thank you, thank you, God;
Thank you, God; thank you, God.
Thank you, God, we pray each day.
Thank you, God, we pray.

2. We love you, love you, love you, God;
   Love you, God; love you, God.
   How wonderful you are, dear God.
   We love you more each day.

54 *Discovering God's Love Songbook*

Discovering God's Love Songbook 55

Lesson 28, Part 2

We Celebrate the Mass

To the tune of "Three Blind Mice"

Cel - e - brate!___ Cel - e - brate!___

Come to the Mass!___ Come to the

Mass!___ We pray, we lis - ten, give thanks to

God For all of the gifts he has giv - en to

us, Es - pe - cial - ly Je - sus, the Son of God. Come

cel - e - brate!___ Cel - e - brate!___

56 *Discovering God's Love Songbook*

Discovering God's Love Songbook 57

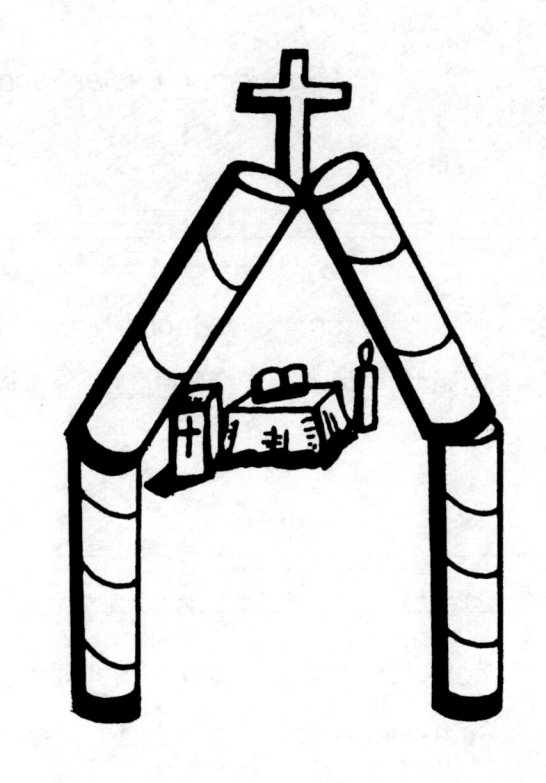

Lesson 29

Goodbye and Hello

To the tunes of
"Goodnight, Ladies" and "Merrily We Roll Along"

Good - bye, Kin - der - gar - ten. Good - bye, kin - der - gar - ten.
Hel — lo, — Sum - mer! Hel — lo, — Sum - mer!

Good-bye, Kin - der - gar - ten, For sum - mer - time is here!
Hel — lo, — Sum - mer! It's good to see you here.

We will play out in the sun, in the sun, in the sun.
God is with us ev - 'ry day, Ev - 'ry day, ev - 'ry day.

D.C. al Coda

We will play out in the sun, For sum - mer - time is here!
God is with us ev - 'ry day And in the night - time, too.

58 *Discovering God's Love Songbook*

Discovering God's Love Songbook 59

Lesson 30, Part 1

Mom

To the tune of "Three Blind Mice"

I love my mom. I love my mom. She loves me too. She loves me too. She's the ni-cest mom that I know. She takes care of me, where-ev-er we go. She helps me learn and she helps me to grow. She's my mom!

60 *Discovering God's Love Songbook*

Dad

To the tune of "Three Blind Mice"

I love my dad. I love my dad. He loves me too. He loves me too. He's the ni-cest man that I know. He takes care of me, where-ev-er we go. He helps me learn and he helps me to grow. He's my dad!

Lesson 30, Part 2

Discovering God's Love Songbook   61

Lesson 31

Mary, Our Mother

To the tune of "Away in a Manger"

Hail, Mar-y, our mo-ther. Hail, Je-sus, your son. You know us and love us. You care for each one! We pray to you, Mar-y, To help us each day. Will you tell dear Je-sus To you both we'll pray?

Yes

62   Discovering God's Love Songbook

A Birthday Song

To the tune of "London Bridge"

You're a special gift of God, Gift of God, gift of God. You're a special gift of God. Happy Birthday!

Discovering God's Love Songbook **63**

Acknowledgments

Original illustrations by Julie Brunet and Renée McAlister, recreated by Arthur Friedman

Copyright © 2000 by William H. Sadlier, Inc. All rights reserved. This book, or any part thereof, may not be reproduced in any form, or by any means, including electronic, photographic, or mechanical, or by any sound recording system, or by any device for storage and retrieval of information, without the written permission of the publisher.

Printed in the United States of America.

S is a registered trademark of William H. Sadlier, Inc.

Home Office:
9 Pine Street
New York, New York 10005–4700

ISBN: 978-0-8215-2478-7
5 6 7 8 9 10 RPP 16 15 14 13